Workshop on Generalization in the Age of Deep Learning 2018

New Orleans, Louisiana, USA
5 June 2018

ISBN: 978-1-5108-6359-0

Printed from e-media with permission by:

Curran Associates, Inc.
57 Morehouse Lane
Red Hook, NY 12571

Some format issues inherent in the e-media version may also appear in this print version.

Printed by Curran Associates, Inc. (2018)

Association for Computational Linguistics
209 N. Eighth Street
Stroudsburg, Pennsylvania 18360

Phone: 1-570-476-8006
Fax: 1-570-476-0860

acl@aclweb.org

Additional copies of this publication are available from:

Curran Associates, Inc.
57 Morehouse Lane
Red Hook, NY 12571 USA
Phone: 845-758-0400
Fax: 845-758-2633
Email: curran@proceedings.com
Web: www.proceedings.com

NAACL HLT 2018

Generalization in the Age of Deep Learning

Proceedings of the Workshop

June 5, 2018
New Orleans, Louisiana

Deep learning has brought a wealth of state-of-the-art results and new capabilities. Although methods have achieved near human-level performance on many benchmarks, numerous recent studies imply that these benchmarks only weakly test their intended purpose, and that simple examples produced either by human or machine, cause systems to fail spectacularly. For example, a recently released textual entailment demo was criticized on social media for predicting that "John killed Mary" entails "Mary killed John" with 92% confidence. Such surprising failures combined with the inability to interpret state-of-the-art models have eroded confidence in our systems, and while these systems are not perfect, the real flaw lies with our benchmarks that do not adequately measure a model's ability to generalize, and are thus easily gameable.

This workshop provides a venue for exploring new approaches for measuring and enforcing generalization in models. We have solicited work in the following areas:

1. Analysis of existing models and their failings.

2. Creation of new evaluation paradigms, e.g. zero-shot learning, Winnograd schema, and datasets that avoid explicit types of gamification.

3. Modeling advances such as regularization, compositionality, interpretability, inductive bias, multi-task learning, and other methods that promote generalization.

Our goals are similar in spirit to those of the recent "Build it Break it" shared task. However, we propose going beyond identifying areas of weakness (i.e. "breaking" existing systems), and discussing evaluations that rigorously test generalization as well as modeling techniques for enforcing it.

We received eight archival submissions and seven cross submission, accepting five archival papers and all cross submission. Predominately papers covered the first two stated goals of workshop, with the majority identifying flaws in either methods or data. Of the papers proposing new evaluations, many explored using synthetic data. The papers will be presented as posters at the workshop and we are excited to see what discussions they generate. In addition to twelve papers that will be presented we are equally excited for talks from Sam Bowman, Yejin Choi, Percy Liang, Ndapa Nakashole, Devi Parikh, and Dan Roth. Finally , we would also like to thank Yejin, Devi and Dan for helping through service on the steering committee.

– Yonatan, Omer, Mark

Organizers:

Yonatan Bisk	University of Washington
Omer Levy	University of Washington
Mark Yatskar	University of Washington

Steering:

Yejin Choi	University of Washington
Dan Roth	University of Pennsylvania
Devi Parikh	Georgia Tech / Facebook AI Research

Program Committee:

Jacob Andreas	UC Berkeley
Antoine Bosselut	U Washington
Kai-Wei Chang	UCLA
Christos Christodoulopoulos	Amazon, Inc
Greg Durrett	UT Austin
Maxwell Forbes	U Washington
Spandana Gella	Edinburgh U
Luheng He	U Washington
Srinivasan Iyer	U Washington
Mohit Iyyer	UMass Amherst
Robin Jia	Stanford U
Ioannis Konstas	Heriot-Watt U
Jonathan Kummerfeld	U Michigan
Alice Lai	UIUC
Mike Lewis	FAIR
Tal Linzen	JHU
Vicente Ordonez	U Virginia
Siva Reddy	Stanford U
Alan Ritter	Ohio State U
Rajhans Samdani	Spoke
Sameer Singh	UC Irvine
Alane Suhr	Cornell U
Chen-Tse Tsai	U Pennsylvania
Shyam Upadhyay	U Pennsylvania
Andreas Vlachos	U Sheffield

Table of Contents

Conference Program

June 5th

9:00–9:15 **Welcome**

9:15–9:50 **Yejin Choi**

9:50–10:25 **Dan Roth**

10:25–10:35 **Break**

10:35–11:10 **Percy Liang**

11:10–11:45 **Ndapa Nakashole**

11:45–12:20 **Hal Daume III**

12:20–13:30 **Lunch**

13:30–14:30 **Poster Session**

Towards Inference-Oriented Reading Comprehension: ParallelQA
Soumya Wadhwa, Varsha Embar, Matthias Grabmair and Eric Nyberg

Commonsense mining as knowledge base completion? A study on the impact of novelty
Stanislaw Jastrzebski, Dzmitry Bahdanau, Seyedarian Hosseini, Michael Noukhovitch, Yoshua Bengio and Jackie Cheung

Deep learning evaluation using deep linguistic processing
Alexander Kuhnle and Ann Copestake

The Fine Line between Linguistic Generalization and Failure in Seq2Seq-Attention Models
Noah Weber, Leena Shekhar and Niranjan Balasubramanian

June 5th (continued)

Extrapolation in NLP
Jeff Mitchell, Pontus Stenetorp, Pasquale Minervini and Sebastian Riedel

14:45–15:20 **Sam Bowman**

15:20–15:55 **Devi Parikh**

15:55–16:10 **Break**

16:10–17:10 **Panel**

17:10–17:15 **Closing**

Towards Inference-Oriented Reading Comprehension: ParallelQA

Soumya Wadhwa* **Varsha Embar*** **Matthias Grabmair** **Eric Nyberg**
Carnegie Mellon University
{soumyaw, vembar, mgrabmai, en09}@andrew.cmu.edu

Abstract

In this paper, we investigate the tendency of end-to-end neural Machine Reading Comprehension (MRC) models to match shallow patterns rather than perform inference-oriented reasoning on RC benchmarks. We aim to test the ability of these systems to answer questions which focus on referential inference. We propose ParallelQA, a strategy to formulate such questions using parallel passages. We also demonstrate that existing neural models fail to generalize well to this setting.

1 Introduction

Reading Comprehension (RC) is the task of reading a body of text and answering questions about it. It requires a deep understanding of the information presented in order to reason about entities, actions, events, and their interrelationships. This necessitates language understanding skills as well as the cognitive ability to draw inferences.

Recent efforts in creating large-scale datasets have triggered a renewed interest in the RC task, with subsequent development of complex end-to-end solutions featuring neural models. While these models do exceedingly well on the specific datasets they are developed for (some reaching or even surpassing human performance), they do not perform proportionally across datasets. Weissenborn et al. (2017) have shown that using a context or type matching heuristic to derive simple neural baseline architectures can achieve comparable results. Our experiments also indicate that pattern matching can work well on these datasets.

Inference, an important RC skill (Spearritt, 1972; Strange, 1980), is the ability to understand the meaning of text without all the information being stated explicitly. Table 5, Section A describes the types of inference that we may encounter while comprehending a passage along with the cues that help perform such reasoning. Although state-of-the-art deep learning models for machine reading are believed to have such reasoning capabilities, the limited ability of these models to generalize indicates certain shortcomings. We believe that it is important to develop benchmarks which give a realistic sense of a system's RC capabilities. Thus, our goal in this paper is two-fold:

Proof of Concept: We propose a method to create an RC dataset that assesses a model's ability to:

- move beyond lexical pattern matching between the question and passage,
- infer the correct answers to questions which contain referring expressions, and
- generalize to different language styles.

Analysis of Existing Models: We test three end-to-end neural MRC models, which perform well on SQuAD (Rajpurkar et al., 2016), on a few question-answer pairs generated using our methodology. We demonstrate that it is indeed difficult for these systems to answer such questions, also indicating their tendencies to resort to shallow pattern matching and overfit to training data.

2 Existing Datasets

In this work, we focus on datasets with multi-word spans as answers rather than cloze-style RC datasets like MCTest (Richardson et al., 2013), CNN / Daily Mail (Hermann et al., 2015) and Children's Book Test (Weston et al., 2015).

The Stanford Question Answering Dataset (SQuAD) (Rajpurkar et al., 2016) was one of the first large scale RC datasets (over 100k QA pairs), where the answer to each question is a span in the given passage. For its collection, different sets of crowd-workers were asked to formulate questions and answers using passages obtained from ~500 Wikipedia articles. However, this resulted in the questions having similar word patterns to the sentences containing the answers. We empirically demonstrate this in Table 1, where we ob-

*Equal Contribution

Proceedings of the Workshop on Generalization in the Age of Deep Learning, pages 1–7
New Orleans, Louisiana, June 5, 2018.

served that the sentence in the passage with the highest lexical similarity to the question contained the answer ~80% of the time. Final answers tend to be short, with an average span length of around 3 tokens, and are largely entities (40.88%). Subramanian et al. (2017) and Yang et al. (2017) provide evidence for regular patterns in candidate answers that neural models can exploit. We show in subsequent sections that models which perform well on SQuAD rely on lexical pattern matching, and are also not robust to variance in language style.

Metric	SQuAD	NewsQA	ParallelQA
Jaccard	79.28%	38.11%	27.45%
TF-IDF	81.32%	51.86%	31.37%
BM25	74.26%	43.45%	27.45%

Table 1: Sentence Retrieval Performance using Jaccard similarity (Jaccard, 1912), TF-IDF overlap (Sparck Jones, 1972) and BM-25 overlap (Robertson et al., 1994) scoring metrics

To alleviate the lack of topic diversity in SQuAD, NewsQA (Trischler et al., 2016) was created from 12,744 news articles sampled from CNN/Daily Mail. To ensure lexical diversity, one set of crowd-workers generated questions using only an abstractive summary, while the answer spans were marked in the full article by another set of crowd-workers. However, news articles tend to encourage questions that point to entities, and the dataset does not specifically focus on inference. Determining the exact answer span is harder, but this may be due to the use of only news highlights to generate questions; this may induce noise in the answer spans marked in the news articles since the question might not be exactly apt.

To prevent annotation bias, SearchQA (Dunn et al., 2017) starts with question-answer pairs from Jeopardy! and adds documents retrieved by a search engine for each question as its context. However, the questions are mostly factoid. Kočiský et al. (2017) found that 80% of answers are bigrams or unigrams, and 99% contain 5 or fewer tokens, with many answers being named entities. TriviaQA (Joshi et al., 2017) similarly includes question-answer pairs authored by trivia enthusiasts along with independently-gathered evidence documents which provide distant supervision for answering the questions.

These datasets have facilitated the development of new QA models, but we believe there are several important aspects of RC that remain untested.

3 ParallelQA

In an RC task, there is a need to incorporate questions that require not just lexical and syntactic prowess, but reference resolution, multiple steps of reasoning, and use of world knowledge. These capabilities ultimately lead to global rather than sentence-level understanding of text. The construction of a large-scale dataset of this nature is a challenging task. We take a small step in this direction by focusing on referential inference.[1] WikiHop (Welbl et al., 2017) is an interesting multi-hop inference-focused dataset created using entity-relation pairs for queries spanning different Wikipedia passages. While the focus of our pilot study is similar to theirs, we believe that our method can easily be extended to other inference types. Also, identifying the correct span is more challenging than choosing an answer from a list.

We aim to incorporate multiple language styles, making it hard for the system to memorize linguistic patterns (Williams et al., 2017). We achieve this by using two parallel passages that talk about the same or related subject(s) but are obtained from different sources. This helps in formulating referential inference questions because there exists no single sentence in the passage which matches a paraphrase of the question, and necessitates that inference (which goes beyond co-reference) be performed across both passages. Evaluation is easy and objective because answers are still spans within the passages. Questions can be answered solely on the basis of the information provided in their accompanying passages.

For example, to answer Question 1 in Table 2, the system will have to infer from passage 1 that President Kamazu Banda belongs to the MCP and was defeated in the elections. The equivalence of this event and the election in passage 2 must be established, while comprehending that the "favored challenger" Bakili Muluzi is the one Banda lost the elections to, and who belonged to the UDP, making it the correct answer.

Given that the information is spatially scattered across the two passages, this method would ensure that the parallel passages have to be understood in combination to answer the question.

[1]Referential inference is the process of identifying the discourse and/or real-world entity referred to by a linguistic expression (name, noun, pronoun, etc.).

Hastings Kamuzu Banda was the leader of Malawi from 1961 to 1994. In 1963 he was formally appointed prime minister of Nyasaland and, a year later, led the country to independence as Malawi. Two years later he proclaimed Malawi a republic with himself as president. He declared Malawi a one-party state under the Malawi Congress Party (MCP) and became President of MCP as well as President for Life of Malawi in 1971. A referendum ended his one-party state and a special assembly ended his life-term presidency, stripping him of most of his powers. Banda ran for president in the democratic elections which followed and was defeated. He died in South Africa in 1997.
Malawians Saturday wound up an historic election campaign bringing multiparty politics to a country ruled for the past three decades by President Hastings Kamuzu Banda. The ailing president inspected troops from an open truck as some 20,000 people turned up at a stadium here to celebrate his official birthday ahead of elections on May 17. Reading a prepared speech with some difficulty, Banda appealed to Malawians to conduct themselves "as ladies and gentlemen" during the elections, which should be "free and fair." Meanwhile, the bigger opposition rally was addressed by the presidential challenger favored to win the elections, Bakili Muluzi of the United Democratic Front (UDF).
Question 1: Who emerged victorious between the MCP and UDF? Question 2: What did the MCP leader ask of the people of Malawi on polling day? Question 3: What brought multiparty politics to Malawi after three decades?

Table 2: Example of a Parallel Passage. The questions and corresponding answers are color coded.

4 Proof of Concept

For a fair evaluation of existing models, we sought to use data drawn from a similar domain, but written in a different style. We chose the CNN/Daily Mail corpus and Wikipedia because they both focus on factoid statements, yet differ in language style to a noticeable extent (e.g. in the use of idiomatic expressions). We picked 20 CNN/Daily Mail articles at random to form one of the passages in our pair. To find an associated parallel passage, we selected the most frequently mentioned entities in each article and obtained its corresponding Wikipedia pages. We fragmented these into passages with at most 500 words, and performed a k-Nearest Neighbor search using tf-idf and topic vectors (Blei et al., 2003) to form pairs. We tuned the number of entities per article used to retrieve Wikipedia pages, as well as the sections considered in each article. This process produced a total of 15 News-Wiki passage pairs. While no two pairs have the same news article, they may be paired with the same Wiki passage.

We focused on referential inference for this pilot, but the method can be extended to include questions based on other types of inference. 15 human annotators were given explicit instructions and real-world examples to form question-answer pairs using given parallel passages. We collected $\sim$ 50 valid question-answer pairs through this mechanism. The average length of the answers obtained was around 4 words. Basic sentence retrieval statistics (similar to the ones discussed in Section 2) are shown in Table 1, indicating that lexical similarity between the question and passage sentences is insufficient to obtain an answer. Our small-scale experiment shows the feasibility of the approach, although collecting a larger dataset requires more effort in acquiring passages and generating questions from diverse sources.

5 Analysis of Existing Models

Model	SQuAD		ParallelQA	
	EM	F1	EM	F1
BiDAF	67.70	77.30	35.29	42.52
DrQA	69.64	78.76	39.22	47.23
R-Net	71.07	79.51	41.18	50.38

Table 3: Performance on SQuAD vs ParallelQA

We consider three deep learning models: Bidirectional Attention Flow (BiDAF) [2] (Seo et al., 2016), Document Reader (DrQA) [3] (Chen et al., 2017), and Gated Self-Matching Networks (R-Net) [4] (Wang et al., 2017) trained on SQuAD. We feed the concatenated parallel passage and the question as inputs. On a total of 51 QA pairs, we observed exact match (EM) scores of about 40% and token overlap F1 scores of about 45% for all models, versus their performance on the SQuAD dataset (EM of almost 70% and F1 of 80%). Detailed results are shown in Table 3.

Although the models were trained and tested on different datasets, we expect them to perform reasonably well on the new task since the data sources and domain are similar. Also, the size of our collected data is much smaller than the SQuAD development set, but we believe that the samples are fairly representative of data that can be generated

[2] https://allenai.github.io/bi-att-flow/

[3] https://github.com/hitvoice/DrQA

[4] https://github.com/HKUST-KnowComp/R-Net

Passage	Question
...The UN is the largest, most familiar, most internationally represented and most powerful intergovernmental organisation in the world...UN envoy Yasushi Akashi called a meeting of all parties to talks on a four-month ceasefire for Saturday afternoon, he added...	Who was sent to Bosnia as the envoy of most powerful intergovernmental organisation in the world?
...On arrival, the president and his wife Hillary were taken to University College, one of 37 Oxford colleges, where he studied political science as a Rhodes Scholar between October 1968 and June 1970... Clinton was born and raised in Arkansas and ...	From which state was this US President who was a Rhodes scholar between 1968 and 1970?
...withdrew from a UN-designated three-kilometer (two-mile) exclusion zone around the eastern Bosnian enclave of Gorazde ... The United Nations (UN) is an intergovernmental organization ... A replacement for the ineffective League of Nations, the organization ... [eastern Bosnian enclave, Gorazde, eastern Bosnian enclave of Gorazde]	Where in Bosnia did the successor of the League of Nations designate an exclusion zone?
Todd Martin squeezed to a 7-6 7-6 victory over fellow-American Pete Sampras in the final of the Queen's Club tournament here on Sunday. The win further bolstered fifth seeded Martin's reputation as one of the most dangerous grass court players...	Pistol Pete lost to whom in the Queen's club tournament?
... (RENAMO) rebels at a UN-supervised assembly point brutally beat one of their senior officials during a mutiny over severance pay on June 1 at Mocubela, about 100 kilometers (62 miles) east of Mocuba. But RENAMO has denied the official, identified as Raul Dique, was beaten up by mutineers, the Mozambican news agency (AIM) said in a report monitored in Harare Thursday ...	Where was Raul Dique beaten up by rebels of RENAMO?

Table 4: Examples of error trends on ParallelQA: blue - gold answer, red - span predicted incorrectly by all models, orange - BiDAF and R-Net prediction overlap, olive - BiDAF, magenta - DrQA, cyan - R-Net

using our proposed mechanism. Thus, the low EM and F1 scores support our hypothesis that these datasets do not adequately assess the capabilities of these models, which overfit to lexical patterns rather than generalizing.

We now discuss a few common errors observed upon manual inspection of the results. Examples for each are provided in Table 4. The distribution of predictions across these error categories can be found in Figure 1, Section A.

- **High Lexical Overlap - Incorrect Sentence**: The models tend to pick answer spans from sentences which have high lexical overlap with the question. We observe that this accounts for the largest chunk of errors across all models (example 2). Our observations are consistent with the findings of Jia and Liang (2017). The models often simply resolve the referential expression in the question to its corresponding entity. In example 1, the models resolve "organisation" in the question to "The UN" due to high lexical similarity.
- **Incorrect Answer Boundaries**: This is the second most frequently observed error, where the answers generated are almost correct, but models face issues in appropriately defining answer boundaries (example 3). R-Net and DrQA, on average, produce shorter answers. BiDAF tends to produce longer answers.
- **Missing Logical Inference**: Models are sometimes unable to make certain logical conclusions like A's victory over B implies that B lost to A (example 4).
- **Entity Type Confusion**: Despite having a variety of entities as answers to questions in the training data, sometimes the model answers do not correspond to the correct entity type (example 5).

6 Discussion & Conclusion

While our approach is promising, we observed a few problems during the pilot study. Longer passages and constraints on the question formulation require more time and skill in the annotation process. This can lead to crowd-workers formulating a single referring expression and then using it in different contexts to form questions, reducing diversity. For some questions, although inference is needed, both passages may not be necessary to answer them. Since we used news articles and Wikipedia passages in our pilot study, 58.82% of answers were named entities. We plan to extend this mechanism to other inference types and conduct a larger pilot before scaling up the collection.

Our experiments demonstrate that the ParallelQA task can be more challenging than some prior QA tasks. Our analysis shows that many popular RC datasets seem to test the ability of models to pick up superficial cues. ParallelQA is our proposed step towards inference-oriented reading comprehension. We use parallel passages from different sources for generating reasoning questions which encourage systems to gain a deeper understanding of language, and become robust to variations in style and topic. We include examples from our initial pilot study in Table 6.

Acknowledgments

The authors would like to thank Chaitanya Malaviya, Sandeep Subramanian, Siddharth Dalmia, Tejas Nama and Vaishnavi AK for useful discussions. We would also like to express our gratitude to the annotators who participated in the pilot study.

References

David M Blei, Andrew Y Ng, and Michael I Jordan. 2003. Latent dirichlet allocation. *Journal of machine Learning research* 3(Jan):993–1022.

Danqi Chen, Adam Fisch, Jason Weston, and Antoine Bordes. 2017. Reading wikipedia to answer open-domain questions. *arXiv preprint arXiv:1704.00051* .

Matthew Dunn, Levent Sagun, Mike Higgins, Ugur Guney, Volkan Cirik, and Kyunghyun Cho. 2017. Searchqa: A new q&a dataset augmented with context from a search engine. *arXiv preprint arXiv:1704.05179* .

Karl Moritz Hermann, Tomas Kocisky, Edward Grefenstette, Lasse Espeholt, Will Kay, Mustafa Suleyman, and Phil Blunsom. 2015. Teaching machines to read and comprehend. In *Advances in Neural Information Processing Systems*. pages 1693–1701.

Paul Jaccard. 1912. The distribution of the flora in the alpine zone. *New phytologist* 11(2):37–50.

Robin Jia and Percy Liang. 2017. Adversarial examples for evaluating reading comprehension systems. *arXiv preprint arXiv:1707.07328* .

Mandar Joshi, Eunsol Choi, Daniel S Weld, and Luke Zettlemoyer. 2017. Triviaqa: A large scale distantly supervised challenge dataset for reading comprehension. *arXiv preprint arXiv:1705.03551* .

Tomáš Kočiský, Jonathan Schwarz, Phil Blunsom, Chris Dyer, Karl Moritz Hermann, Gábor Melis, and Edward Grefenstette. 2017. The narrativeqa reading comprehension challenge. *arXiv preprint arXiv:1712.07040* .

Pranav Rajpurkar, Jian Zhang, Konstantin Lopyrev, and Percy Liang. 2016. Squad: 100,000+ questions for machine comprehension of text. *arXiv preprint arXiv:1606.05250* .

Matthew Richardson, Christopher JC Burges, and Erin Renshaw. 2013. Mctest: A challenge dataset for the open-domain machine comprehension of text. In *Proceedings of the 2013 Conference on Empirical Methods in Natural Language Processing*. pages 193–203.

Stephen E Robertson, Steve Walker, Susan Jones, Micheline Hancock-Beaulieu, and Mike Gatford. 1994. Okapi at trec-3 proceedings of the third text retrieval conference. TREC.

Minjoon Seo, Aniruddha Kembhavi, Ali Farhadi, and Hannaneh Hajishirzi. 2016. Bidirectional attention flow for machine comprehension. *arXiv preprint arXiv:1611.01603* .

Karen Sparck Jones. 1972. A statistical interpretation of term specificity and its application in retrieval. *Journal of documentation* 28(1):11–21.

Donald Spearritt. 1972. Identification of sub-skills of reading comprehension by maximum likelihood factor analysis1. *ETS Research Bulletin Series* pages i–24.

Michael Strange. 1980. Instructional implications of a conceptual theory of reading comprehension. *The Reading Teacher* 33:391–97.

Sandeep Subramanian, Tong Wang, Xingdi Yuan, and Adam Trischler. 2017. Neural models for key phrase detection and question generation. *arXiv preprint arXiv:1706.04560* .

Adam Trischler, Tong Wang, Xingdi Yuan, Justin Harris, Alessandro Sordoni, Philip Bachman, and Kaheer Suleman. 2016. Newsqa: A machine comprehension dataset. *arXiv preprint arXiv:1611.09830* .

Wenhui Wang, Nan Yang, Furu Wei, Baobao Chang, and Ming Zhou. 2017. Gated self-matching networks for reading comprehension and question answering. In *Proceedings of the 55th Annual Meeting of the Association for Computational Linguistics (Volume 1: Long Papers)*. volume 1, pages 189–198.

Dirk Weissenborn, Georg Wiese, and Laura Seiffe. 2017. Fastqa: A simple and efficient neural architecture for question answering. *arXiv preprint arXiv:1703.04816* .

Johannes Welbl, Pontus Stenetorp, and Sebastian Riedel. 2017. Constructing datasets for multi-hop reading comprehension across documents. *arXiv preprint arXiv:1710.06481* .

Jason Weston, Antoine Bordes, Sumit Chopra, Alexander M Rush, Bart van Merriënboer, Armand Joulin, and Tomas Mikolov. 2015. Towards ai-complete question answering: A set of prerequisite toy tasks. *arXiv preprint arXiv:1502.05698* .

Adina Williams, Nikita Nangia, and Samuel R Bowman. 2017. A broad-coverage challenge corpus for sentence understanding through inference. *arXiv preprint arXiv:1704.05426* .

Zhilin Yang, Junjie Hu, Ruslan Salakhutdinov, and William W Cohen. 2017. Semi-supervised qa with generative domain-adaptive nets. *arXiv preprint arXiv:1702.02206* .

A Supplemental Material

Inference Type	Meaning	Examples	Information Required
Referential	Coreferences, Referring Expressions	Bill Clinton's wife is Hillary Clinton	A link between the expression and entity it refers to
Figurative	Metaphors	All the world's a stage	A dictionary of common metaphors and what they mean
Part-Whole	Inclusion	A dog is an animal	An ontology of hierarchical and other relationships between words
Numeric	Units, Operations	60 seconds is a minute	Equivalence (and conversion) of units, Basic Operation Skills
Lexical	Meanings from Linguistic Context	I ate an apple (apple = fruit or company?)	Contextual Information: Word Embeddings / NER / PoS
Denotation	Literal Meanings of Expressions	Olive branch denotes peace	World Knowledge + Contextual Information
Spatial	Reasoning about Space	Berlin is in Germany which is in Europe	World Knowledge + Basic Spatial Reasoning Rules
Temporal	Reasoning about Time	World War II happened before Cold War	World Knowledge + Basic Temporal Reasoning Rules

Table 5: Different Types of Inference along with examples and possible information required to perform them

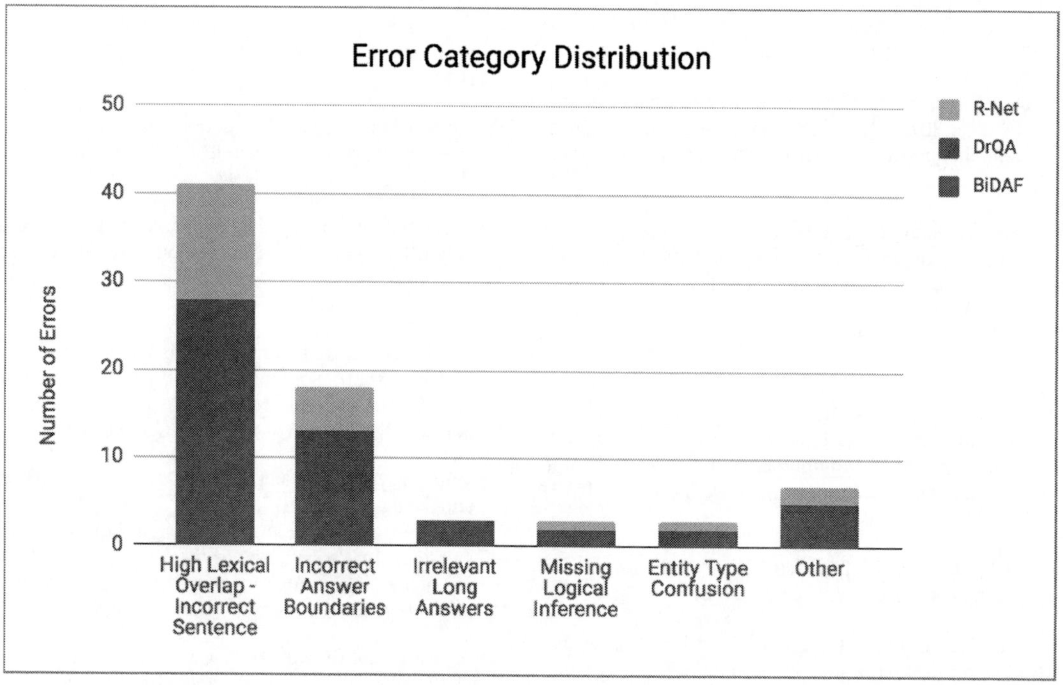

Figure 1: Distribution of errors by BiDAF, DrQA and R-Net across different categories using manual inspection

Todd Martin squeezed to a 7-6 7-6 victory over fellow-American Pete Sampras in the final of the Queen's Club tournament here on Sunday. The win further bolstered fifth seeded Martin's reputation as one of the most dangerous grass court players. But it was essentially a baseline slogging match which provided little to whet the appetite for Wimbledon. There were no breaks of serve in either set and only three break points in the entire match - two against Sampras in the second game and one against Martin in the next. Martin clinched the first tie-break courtesy of a double fault from Sampras to lead 4-2 and then a glorious cross-court forehand return on his second set point to take the shoot-out 7-4. He took the second tie-break by the same score, Sampras saving three match points before a fierce smash clinched Martin's third career title and his first victory over his compatriot in four meetings.

Petros "Pete" Sampras (born August 12, 1971) is a retired American tennis player widely regarded as one of the greatest in the history of the sport. He was a longtime world No. 1 with a precise serve that earned him the nickname "Pistol Pete". His career began in 1988 and ended at the 2002 US Open, which he won, defeating rival Andre Agassi in the final. Sampras was the first man to win 14 Grand Slam singles titles (seven Wimbledon, five US Open, two Australian Open). He also won seven year-end championships and finished six consecutive seasons atop the rankings. Summary of professional awards. U.S. Olympic Committee "Sportsman of the Year" in 1997. He was the first tennis player to receive this award. GQ Magazine's Individual Athlete Award for Man of the Year in 2000. Selected the No. 1 player (of 25 players) in the past 25 years by a panel of 100 current and past players, journalists, and tournament directors to commemorate the 25th anniversary of the ATP in 1997. Voted 48th athlete of Top 50 Greatest North American Athletes of ESPN's SportsCentury (also youngest on list). In 2005, TENNIS Magazine named Sampras the greatest tennis player for the period 1965 through 2005, from its list, "The 40 Greatest Players of the TENNIS Era".

Question 1: The first man to win 14 Grand Slam singles titles lost to whom in the Queen's club tournament?

Question 2: The greatest tennis player for the period 1965 through 2005 lost to Todd Martin in the finals of which tournament?

Question 3: What was the tally of Todd's career titles after defeating the GQ Magazine's Man of the Year award winner, in the final of Queen's club tournament?

Cambodian co-premiers Prince Norodom Ranariddh and Hun Sen said Wednesday they had agreed to holding peace talks with the Khmer Rouge in Pyongyang without preconditions, in response to an appeal by King Norodom Sihanouk. The co-premiers had sent an official letter to the king "saying that we are ready to go to Pyongyang without ceasefire, without preconditions," Prince Ranariddh told journalists. "Let talks begin," he added. Hun Sen said the talks, beginning on May 27, would be based on a peace plan put forward by King Sihanouk, but added that the government had yet to receive a reply from the Khmer Rouge regarding the proposal. King Sihanouk has proposed that certain "acceptable" members of the Khmer Rouge be given senior cabinet posts in the government in exchange for giving up their zones, ceasing all guerrilla activities and merging their fighters with the royal armed forces.

Hun Sen is the Prime Minister of Cambodia, President of the Cambodian People's Party (CPP), and Member of Parliament (MP) for Kandal. He has served as Prime Minister since 1985, making him the longest serving head of government of Cambodia, and one of the longest serving leaders in the world. From 1979 to 1986 and again from 1987 to 1990, Hun Sen served as Cambodia's foreign minister. His full honorary title is Samdech Akeak Moha Sena Padey Techo Hun Sen. Born Hun Bunal, he changed his name to Hun Sen in 1972 two years after joining the Khmer Rouge. Hun Sen rose to the premiership in January 1985 when the one-party National Assembly appointed him to succeed Chan Sy who had died in office in December 1984. He held the position until the 1993 UN-backed elections, which resulted in a hung parliament. After contentious negotiations with the FUNCINPEC, Hun Sen was accepted as Second Prime Minister, serving alongside Norodom Ranariddh until a 1997 coup which toppled the latter. Ung Huot was then selected to succeed Ranariddh.

Question 1: According to Hun Bunal, what is the basis of talks on May 27th?

Question 2: Until which year did the Cambodian co-premiers hold office?

Question 3: The President of the Cambodian People's Party was holding peace talks with the Khmer Rouge along with whom?

Table 6: Examples of collected parallel passages. The questions and corresponding answers are color coded.

Commonsense mining as knowledge base completion? A study on the impact of novelty

Stanisław Jastrzębski*
Jagiellonian University
stanislaw.jastrzebski@uj.edu.pl

Dzmitry Bahdanau
MILA
Université de Montréal

Seyedarian Hosseini
MILA
Université de Montréal

Michael Noukhovitch
MILA
Université de Montréal

Yoshua Bengio†
MILA
Université de Montréal

Jackie Chi Kit Cheung
MILA
McGill University

Abstract

Commonsense knowledge bases such as ConceptNet represent knowledge in the form of relational triples. Inspired by recent work by (Li et al., 2016), we analyse if knowledge base completion models can be used to mine commonsense knowledge from raw text. We propose *novelty* of predicted triples with respect to the training set as an important factor in interpreting results. We critically analyse the difficulty of mining novel commonsense knowledge, and show that a simple baseline method outperforms the previous state of the art on predicting more novel triples.

1 Introduction

Many natural language understanding tasks require commonsense knowledge in order to resolve ambiguities involving implicit assumptions. Collecting such knowledge and representing it in a reusable way is thus an important challenge. There exist several commonsense knowledge bases maintained by experts (CyC) or acquired by crowdsourcing (ConceptNet) which represent commonsense knowledge as relational triples (e.g., *("pen", "UsedFor", "writing")*) (Liu and Singh, 2004). Automatic mining of commonsense knowledge, the focus of this work, aims to improve the coverage of such resources.

One common way of improving the coverage of knowledge bases is through knowledge base completion (KBC), which can be formalized as predicting the existence of edges between (usually) pre-existing nodes in the graph. Recent work by Li et al. (2016) approached commonsense mining as a KBC task. Their method mines candidate triples from Wikipedia and reranks the triples with a KBC model in order to extend ConceptNet.

The goal of this paper is to investigate why recent systems such as the above achieve good performance, and understand their potential for mining commonsense. We approach it by breaking down the previously reported aggregate results into the cases in which models perform well or poorly. We focus in particular on the issue of the *novelty* of model predictions with respect to the triples in the training set. For example, a triple predicted by a system could be correct because it generates output with a slightly different wording or morphological inflection (e.g., *("fish", "AtLocation", "water")* from *("fish", "AtLocation", "in water")*), or it could be correct because it exhibits some degree of semantic generalization (e.g., *("fish", "IsCapableOf", "swimming")* from *("fish", "AtLocation", "in water")*). Arguably, the former could be handled by better standardization of data set formats or more comprehensive model pre-processing, whereas the latter presents an example of genuine commonsense inference and novelty. This analysis is especially important for commonsense mining because of the diversity of the entities, relations, and linguistic expressions thereof in current datasets.

The contribution of this paper is two-fold. First, we test if the KBC task as it is set up in recent work can gauge a model's ability to mine novel commonsense (i.e. find novel commonsense facts based on some resource). We observe the contrary. We present a model that performs poorly on KBC but matches the best model on the task of mining novel commonsense (evaluated by re-ranking extracted candidate triples from Wikipedia). We then examine the cause of this discrepancy, and

*Work partially done as intern in MILA
†CIFAR Senior Fellow

Proceedings of the Workshop on Generalization in the Age of Deep Learning, pages 8–16
New Orleans, Louisiana, June 5, 2018. ©2018 Association for Computational Linguistics

find that around 60% of triples in the KBC test set used by Li et al. (2016) are minor rewordings of existing triples in the training set. This suggests that controlling for the novelty of triples in both KBC and Wikipedia evaluation is needed.

Second, we present a reassessment of previous methods in which we control the dataset for novelty, extending the results of Li et al. (2016). We introduce a simple automated novelty metric and show that it correlates with human judgment. We then show that the performance of most models on both KBC and Wikipedia triple reranking drops drastically when we evaluate them examples that are genuinely new according to our metric. Finally, we demonstrate that a simple baseline model that does not model all interactions between elements in a triple performs surprisingly well on both KBC and reranking when we focus on novel triples.

2 Related work

Knowledge extraction from text corpora is a vast research area (Banko et al., 2007; Mitchell et al., 2015), yet work that targets commonsense knowledge specifically are comparatively rare (Gordon, 2014). Our focus is on the specific approach to mining commonsense knowledge by casting it as a KBC task, as in Li et al. (2016); Forbes and Choi (2017).

Knowledge base completion (KBC) is a method to improve coverage of knowledge base by predicting non-existing edges between nodes (Nickel and Tresp, 2011; Socher et al., 2013). A common modeling approach to KBC is to embed nodes and the edge into a common representation space, followed by a simple prediction model (Socher et al., 2013).

Recently, Dettmers et al. (2017) observed that some KBC benchmarks have test set triples that are simply inversions of triples in their training sets. Our work draws attention to a related issue in commonsense KBC. Additionally, we find that simple baseline models achieve strong performances in our setting, in agreement with other studies of KBC Joulin et al. (2017); Kadlec et al. (2017).

In Angeli and Manning (2013), triple retrieval based on distributional similarity is used to complete ConceptNet. Our procedure for determining the novelty of the triple is similar to methods used in that work, but we apply it only in the context of evaluation.

3 Completion vs Mining

Our goal in this section is to analyse the relation between KBC and commonsense mining tasks following setup of Li et al. (2016).

3.1 Models

All our models take (h, r, t) triples as inputs, where h and t are sequences of words representing concepts and r is a relation from the ConceptNet schema, and output the probability of the triple to be true. Following Li et al. (2016), we embed h and t by computing the sums $\mathbf{h}$ and $\mathbf{t}$ of the respective word vectors.

Levy et al. (2015) showed that in the context of predicting the hypernymy relation using only head or only tail can be a strong baseline. To better understand how complex reasoning is needed for both KBC and mining tasks, we similarly consider the two following models, which make strong simplifying assumptions about the dependencies between elements in a triple. The **Factorized** model uses only two-way interactions to compute the triple score:

$$\begin{aligned} s(\mathbf{h}, \mathbf{r}, \mathbf{t}) = \alpha\langle \mathbf{Ah} + \mathbf{b_1}, \mathbf{Bt} + \mathbf{b_2}\rangle \\ + \beta\langle \mathbf{Ar} + \mathbf{b_1}, \mathbf{Bt} + \mathbf{b_2}\rangle \\ + \gamma\langle \mathbf{Ar} + \mathbf{b_1}, \mathbf{Bh} + \mathbf{b_2}\rangle, \end{aligned} \quad (1)$$

where $\mathbf{h}$, $\mathbf{r}$, and $\mathbf{t}$ are d_1 dimensional embeddings of head, relation and tail, $\mathbf{A}, \mathbf{B}$ are $d_1 \times d_2$ matrices, $\mathbf{b_1}, \mathbf{b_2}$ are d_2 dimensional biases, and α, β, γ are learned scalars. The **Prototypical** model is similar, but considers only the head-to-relation and tail-to-relation terms (first and third terms in Eq. 1).

We compare the two new models with the best model from Li et al. (2016), a single hidden layer **DNN**. In that model, the triple score is computed as:

$$\begin{aligned} u(\mathbf{h}, \mathbf{t}) = \phi(\mathbf{Ah} + \mathbf{Bt} + \mathbf{b_1}) \\ s(\mathbf{h}, \mathbf{r}, \mathbf{t}) = \mathbf{W}u(\mathbf{h}, \mathbf{t}) + \mathbf{b_2}, \end{aligned} \quad (2)$$

where ϕ is a nonlinearity, $\mathbf{A}, \mathbf{B}$ are $d_1 \times d_2$ matrices, $\mathbf{b_1}$ is a d_2 dimensional bias, W is a d_2 dimensional vector and $\mathbf{b_2}$ is a scalar. Additionally, we compare against **Bilinear** of Li et al. (2016)[1]. Bilinear model computes the triple score as:

$$s(\mathbf{h}, r, \mathbf{t}) = \mathbf{h}^{\mathrm{T}}\mathbf{M}_r\mathbf{t}, \quad (3)$$

[1]It is the only model evaluated against the Wikipedia ranking task in Li et al. (2016).

where $\mathbf{M}_r$ is a $d_1 \times d_1$ dimensional matrix, separate for each relation in the dataset. All models' scores are fed into a sigmoid function in order to compute the final prediction.

3.2 Setup

KBC models are trained using $100,000$ triples from ConceptNet5 (Speer and Havasi, 2012) that were extracted from the Open Mind Common Sense (OMCS) corpus (Speer and Havasi, 2012). For evaluation, we consider two ways to split the dataset: a random split, as well as the confidence-based split proposed by (Li et al., 2016), which uses triples with the highest ConceptNet confidence scores as a test set[2]. Following Li et al. (2016) negative examples are sampled by randomly swapping head, tail or relation component of each triple. The cross-entropy loss is used, and models are evaluated using F1 score[3]. All models are initialized using skip-gram embeddings that were pretrained on the OMCS corpus.

The commonsense mining task is based on a set of $1.7M$ extracted candidate triples from Wikipedia by Li et al. (2016). The extracted triples are ranked using a KBC model, and the top of the ranking is manually evaluated. We will refer to the experiments in which we rerank external candidate triples as *mining* experiments.

We found that similar hyperparameters and optimization methods work well across the models. We use $1,000$ hidden units, and apply L2 regularization with a weight of 10^{-6} to the word embeddings. All models are optimized using Adagrad (Duchi et al., 2010) with a learning rate 0.01 and batch sizes of 200 (DNN) and 600 (Factorized and Prototypical). In Section 3.3, we compare against the scores of a Bilinear model provided by Li et al. (2016). Experiments are performed using Keras (Chollet et al., 2015) and TensorFlow (Abadi et al., 2015).

3.3 Comparison of KBC and Wikipedia evaluations

First, we directly test if the performance of a model on the KBC task is predictive of its performance on the mining task. We follow the mining evaluation protocol from (Li et al., 2016): we rank triples by assigned scores and manually evaluate the top 100 resulting triples on a scale from 0 (nonsensical) to 4 (true statement). We re-evaluate their model against our baselines and find that the knowledge base completion task is a poor indicator of performance on Wikipedia. Even though the Factorized and Prototypical models achieve the same or much worse score than DNN on the KBC task (see the first row of Table 1), their mining performance on the top 100 triples is better (than both DNN and Bilinear), see Table 2. Triples were scored by two students and scores were averaged, with 0.81 Pearson correlation and 0.48 kappa inter-annotator agreement.

Novelty \ Model	DNN	Factorized	Prototypical
Entire	**0.892**	0.890	0.794
$\leq 33\%$	**0.950**	0.922	0.911
$(33\%, 66\%]$	**0.920**	0.898	0.839
$\geq 66\%$	0.720	**0.821**	0.574

Table 1: F1 scores on Li et al. (2016) confidence-based test set. F1 score is reported on each bucket (based on the percentile of triple novelty) and the entire test set.

	Bilinear	Factorized	Prototypical	DNN
Wikipedia	2.04	**2.61**	2.55	2.5

Table 2: Average human assigned score (from 1 to 5) of the top 100 Wikipedia triples ranked by baselines compared to DNN and Bilinear from Li et al. (2016).

3.4 Novelty of triples

We hypothesize that the discrepancy reported in Section 3.3 is due to a strong overlap of the training and testing sets in the KBC setup of Li et al. (2016). We perform a human evaluation of the novelty of the triples in the three test sets with respect to the $100,000$ ConceptNet training set used. The first is the confidence-based test set used in Li et al. (2016). We compare it with a random subset of ConceptNet. Finally, we consider a sample of 300 triples from the top $10,000$ triples of Wikipedia dataset ordered by the Bilinear model.

For each triple in the three datasets, we fetch the five closest neighbours using word embedding distance and categorize them into five categories based on the closest triple found in the training set: *"same relation and minor rewording"* (1), *"dif-*

[2]We note that random test set consists of worse quality triples than confidence-based split. However, the latter leads to a serious bias in evaluation. We leave addressing this trade-off for future work.

[3]The threshold is selected based on a separate development set, as in (Speer and Havasi, 2012).

ferent relation and minor rewording" (2), *"same relation and related word"* (3), *"different relation and related word"* (4), *"no directly related triple"* (5). We ignore a small percentage of triples that are not describing commonsense knowledge, as well as false triples (some in the random subset, and a large percentage in the Wikipedia dataset).

To give a better intuition, we provide example triples for the confidence-based split of Li et al. (2016). In Category 1 (defined as "same relation and minor rewording"), we find *("egg", "IsA", "food")*, which has a close analog in the training set: *("egg", "IsA", "type of food")*. An example of a test triple in Category 3 (defined as *"different relation and related word"*) is *("floor", "UsedFor", "walk on")*, which has a corresponding triple in the training set *("floor", "UsedFor", "stand on")*. In the Appendix, we provide more examples of triples from each category.

As shown in Table 3, we observe that approximately 87% examples in the confidence-based test set fall into the first or second category, while these categories constitute only 19% of the considered subset of the Wikipedia triples (even after filtering out false triples). We argue that not controlling for the novelty of triples might introduce hard-to-predict biases in the evaluation.

Finally, to understand the effects of using the confidence-based split, we also re-evaluate models on a random split. We observe that scores are consistently lower than on the confidence-based split (compare the first rows of Tables 1 and 4). Interestingly, the overall performance of the DNN model degrades the most (absolute difference in F1 score 9%), compared to Prototypical (4%) and Factorized (7%).

Dataset \ Novelty	1	2	3	4	5
Wikipedia	14%	5%	17%	8%	44%
Confident	65%	22%	4%	4%	2%
Random	21%	10%	16%	3%	29%

Table 3: Human assigned novelty categories to triples from 3 different test datasets. High quality triples are usually trivial. Each column reports percentage of triples in each category ordered by novelty. Category 1 corresponds to *"same relation and minor rewording"*. Category 5 corresponds to *"no directly related triple"*.

4 Evaluation using novelty metric

Motivated by the described similarity of train and test sets in the KBC task, we shift our attention to re-evaluating models on datasets controlled for novelty, extending results of Li et al. (2016). We consider the same tasks as in Sec. 3: ConceptNet5 completion task and commonsense mining task based on Wikipedia triples.

4.1 Automatically measuring novelty

To approximate novelty, we use word embeddings (computed over the OMCS corpus) to calculate distance $d(a, b) = ||head(a) - head(b)||_2 + ||tail(a) - tail(b)||_2$, where head and tail are represented by the average of word embeddings. Such a formulation is related to the concept of *paradigmatic* similarity (Sahlgren, 2006), and word embedding-based distance can approximate paradigmatic similarity (Sun et al., 2015). Two words are paradigmatically similar if one can be replaced for the other, while maintaining syntactical correctness of the sentence (e.g. *"The wolf/tiger is a fierce animal"*). We observe that many trivial test triples are characterized by the existence of a triple in the training set that only differs by such substitutions.

We observe that the proposed distance metric is correlated with human assigned novelty scores (from Sec. 3.4). On the considered datasets Pearson correlation between automatic novelty score and human assigned novelty score is 0.22 to 0.47, with p-values between 0.03 and 0.004. We acknowledge that the automated metric is simplistic, for instance it underperforms for the triples containing rare words or long phrases. Nevertheless, the metric enables detecting a substantial portion of trivial triples (e.g. morphological variations), and we leave for future work developing better measures of novelty.

Using the introduced metric, we can partially explain the inconsistency in the performance of Prototypical and Bilinear models between KBC and mining Wikipedia. We note that the top of the ranking on Wikipedia consists of mostly very far (novel) triples (Figure 1), while KBC confidence-based test set is mostly composed of trivial triples (as argued in Section 3.4).

4.2 Novelty-binned evaluation of KBC

We now re-evaluate the KBC models using our proposed novelty metric. First, we examine the performance on different subsets of the

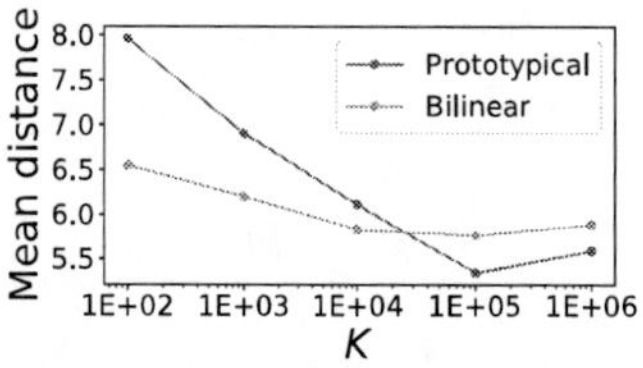

Figure 1: Mean embedding distance (y axis) of top K (x axis) of triples in Wikipedia dataset for Bilinear (orange) and Prototypical (blue).

Novelty \ Model	DNN	Factorized	Prototypical
Entire	0.809	**0.822**	0.755
$\leq 33\%$	**0.883**	0.874	0.866
$(33\%, 66\%]$	0.809	**0.812**	0.758
$\geq 66\%$	0.725	**0.731**	0.674

Table 4: F1 scores on random split. F1 score is reported on each bucket (based on the percentile of triple novelty) and the entire set.

confidence-based split of ConceptNet5. Specifically, we split the confidence-based test set into 3 buckets, according to 33% (1.93 distance) and 66% (2.80 distance) quantile of distance to the training set. Second, we run a similar experiment but on a random split of the training set (bucket thresholds at 2.1 and 2.95). Results are reported in Tables 1 and 4.

As expected, the performance of models degrades quickly across buckets. The performance on the farthest bucket drops from 10 to 20% F1 score with respect to the performance on the closest bucket. We observe that the Factorized model achieves the strongest performance on the farthest bucket.

4.3 Novelty-binned evaluation on Wikipedia

Similar to Section 4.2, we analyse splitting candidate triples for the mining task using our novelty metric. We split the Wikipedia dataset into 3 buckets based on 33% (3.21 distance) and 66% (4.22 distance) quantiles of distance to the training set, and we manually score the top 100 triples in each bucket on the same scale from 1 to 5.

As in Section 4.2, we note a degradation of performance across buckets for all models (from 1.06 to 0.32 mean human assigned score) and again the Factorized model achieves the best performance on the farthest bucket (mean score 2.26 compared to 1.63 and 1.41). The Factorized model outperforms DNN on all buckets despite being a simpler model, which we hypothesize is due to DNN being more prone to overfitting.

Novelty \ Model	DNN	Factorized	Prototypical
$\leq 33\%$	2.47	**2.58**	2.33
$(33\%, 66\%]$	2.34	**2.41**	2.24
$\geq 66\%$	1.41	**2.26**	1.63

Table 5: Novelty based evaluation of quality of mined triples from Wikipedia dataset. Triples are scored by humans on scale from 1 to 5.

5 Conclusions

Mining genuinely novel commonsense is a challenging task, and training successful models will require large training sets (e.g. ConceptNet) and principled evaluation. We critically assessed the potential of KBC models for mining commonsense knowledge, and proposed several first steps towards a more principled evaluation methodology. Future work could focus on developing better novelty metrics, and developing new regularization techniques to better generalize to novel triples.

Acknowledgments

SJ was supported by Grant No. DI 2014/016644 from Ministry of Science and Higher Education, Poland. Work at MILA was funded by NSERC, CIFAR and Canada Research Chairs.

References

Martín Abadi et al. 2015. TensorFlow: Large-scale machine learning on heterogeneous systems. Software available from tensorflow.org. https://www.tensorflow.org/.

Gabor Angeli and Christopher Manning. 2013. Philosophers are mortal: Inferring the truth of unseen facts. In *Proceedings of the Seventeenth Conference on Computational Natural Language Learning*. Association for Computational Linguistics, Sofia, Bulgaria, pages 133–142. http://www.aclweb.org/anthology/W13-3515.

Michele Banko, Michael J. Cafarella, Stephen Soderland, Matthew Broadhead, and Oren Etzioni. 2007. Open Information Extraction from the Web. In *IJCAI*. volume 7, pages 2670–2676. http://www.aaai.org/Papers/IJCAI/2007/IJCAI07-429.pdf.

François Chollet et al. 2015. Keras. https://github.com/keras-team/keras.

Tim Dettmers, Pasquale Minervini, Pontus Stenetorp, and Sebastian Riedel. 2017. Convolutional 2d knowledge graph embeddings. *CoRR* abs/1707.01476. http://arxiv.org/abs/1707.01476.

John Duchi, Elad Hazan, and Yoram Singer. 2010. Adaptive subgradient methods for online learning and stochastic optimization. Technical Report UCB/EECS-2010-24, EECS Department, University of California, Berkeley. http://www2.eecs.berkeley.edu/Pubs/TechRpts/2010/EECS-2010-24.html.

Maxwell Forbes and Yejin Choi. 2017. Verb physics: Relative physical knowledge of actions and objects. In *Proceedings of the 55th Annual Meeting of the Association for Computational Linguistics, ACL 2017, Vancouver, Canada, July 30 - August 4, Volume 1: Long Papers*. pages 266–276. https://doi.org/10.18653/v1/P17-1025.

Jonathan Gordon. 2014. *Inferential Commonsense Knowledge from Text*. Ph.D. thesis.

Armand Joulin, Edouard Grave, Piotr Bojanowski, Maximilian Nickel, and Tomas Mikolov. 2017. Fast linear model for knowledge graph embeddings. *CoRR* abs/1710.10881. http://arxiv.org/abs/1710.10881.

Rudolf Kadlec, Ondrej Bajgar, and Jan Kleindienst. 2017. Knowledge base completion: Baselines strike back. In *Proceedings of the 2nd Workshop on Representation Learning for NLP, Rep4NLP@ACL 2017, Vancouver, Canada, August 3, 2017*. pages 69–74. https://aclanthology.info/papers/W17-2609/w17-2609.

Omer Levy, Steffen Remus, Chris Biemann, and Ido Dagan. 2015. Do supervised distributional methods really learn lexical inference relations? In *Proceedings of the 2015 Conference of the North American Chapter of the Association for Computational Linguistics: Human Language Technologies*. pages 970–976.

Xiang Li, Aynaz Taheri, Lifu Tu, and Kevin Gimpel. 2016. Commonsense knowledge base completion. In *Proceedings of the 54th Annual Meeting of the Association for Computational Linguistics (Volume 1: Long Papers)*. Association for Computational Linguistics, pages 1445–1455. https://doi.org/10.18653/v1/P16-1137.

H. Liu and P. Singh. 2004. Conceptnet: A practical commonsense reasoning tool-kit. *BT Technology Journal* 22(4):211–226. https://doi.org/10.1023/B:BTTJ.0000047600.45421.6d.

T. Mitchell, W. Cohen, E. Hruscha, P. Talukdar, J. Betteridge, A. Carlson, B. Dalvi, M. Gardner, B. Kisiel, J. Krishnamurthy, N. Lao, K. Mazaitis, T. Mohammad, N. Nakashole, E. Platanios, A. Ritter, M. Samadi, B. Settles, R. Wang, D. Wijaya, A. Gupta, X. Chen, A. Saparov, M. Greaves, and J. Welling. 2015. Never-ending learning. In *AAAI*. : Never-Ending Learning in AAAI-2015. http://www.cs.cmu.edu/~wcohen/pubs.html.

Maximilian Nickel and Volker Tresp. 2011. A three-way model for collective learning on multi-relational data. In *In Proceedings of the 28th Intl Conf. on Mach. Learn.* Citeseer.

Magnus Sahlgren. 2006. *The Word-Space Model: Using Distributional Analysis to Represent Syntagmatic and Paradigmatic Relations between Words in High-Dimensional Vector Spaces*. Ph.D. thesis, Stockholm University, Stockholm, Sweden.

Richard Socher, Danqi Chen, Christopher D Manning, and Andrew Ng. 2013. Reasoning With Neural Tensor Networks for Knowledge Base Completion. In C. J. C. Burges, L. Bottou, M. Welling, Z. Ghahramani, and K. Q. Weinberger, editors, *Advances in Neural Information Processing Systems 26*, Curran Associates, Inc., pages 926–934.

Robert Speer and Catherine Havasi. 2012. Representing general relational knowledge in conceptnet 5. In Nicoletta Calzolari (Conference Chair), Khalid Choukri, Thierry Declerck, Mehmet Uğur Doğan, Bente Maegaard, Joseph Mariani, Asuncion Moreno, Jan Odijk, and Stelios Piperidis, editors, *Proceedings of the Eight International Conference on Language Resources and Evaluation (LREC'12)*. European Language Resources Association (ELRA), Istanbul, Turkey.

Fei Sun, Jiafeng Guo, Yanyan Lan, Jun Xu, and Xueqi Cheng. 2015. Learning word representations by jointly modeling syntagmatic and paradigmatic relations. In *Proceedings of the 53rd Annual Meeting of the Association for Computational Linguistics and the 7th International Joint Conference on Natural Language Processing (Volume 1: Long Papers)*. Association for Computational Linguistics, pages 136–145. http://aclweb.org/anthology/P15-1014.

A Example triples

In this Appendix we report randomly picked examples from human assigned novelty categories considered in the paper for each of the 3 datasets. Due to large size of the training set, instead of showing all triples from train set to human annotator, we show only 5 closest using embedding based distance. A triple is classified as belonging to the given category if *at least one* of the retrieved triples is sufficiently related. For example, if for *("egg", "IsA", "food")* we find triple *("egg", "IsA", "type of food")* in the top 5 closest examples, we categorize it as belonging to the first category ("same rel, rephrase").

A.1 Confidence-based split

In this Section we report examples for novelty category from Confidence-based split dataset. For each example we include the 5 examples that were shown to the human annotator, ordered by closeness according to our word embedding metric.

A.1.1 "same rel, rephrase"

- (egg, IsA, food) : *(egg, UsedFor, food), (egg, HasProperty, good for food), (egg, IsA, type of food), (egg, HasProperty, good for you), (egg, AtLocation, omletts),*
- (book, AtLocation, classroom) : *(lot book, AtLocation, classroom), (physic, AtLocation, classroom), (teacher aide, AtLocation, classroom), (desk and chair, AtLocation, classroom), (test paper, AtLocation, classroom),*
- (dog, CapableOf, be pet) : *(dog, CapableOf, be great pet), (dog, CapableOf, be loyal pet), (dog, CapableOf, be over-fed), (dog, IsA, good pet), (dog, NotDesires, be with cat),*

A.1.2 "different rel, rephrase"

- (window, MadeOf, glass) : *(window, HasProperty, make of glass), (window, DefinedAs, glass that be stick to window frame), (abottle, MadeOf, glass), (window, UsedFor, look out of), (window, UsedFor, look inside),*
- (bury cat, HasSubevent, dig hole) : *(bury cat, HasFirstSubevent, dig hole), (bury cat, HasSubevent, dig), (bury cat, HasFirstSubevent, dig grind), (bury cat, UsedFor, when your cat be dead), (bury cat, HasPrerequisite, make sure it be dead),*
- (bridge, UsedFor, cross river) : *(bridge, CapableOf, cross river), (bridge, UsedFor, cross sometihng), (bridge, UsedFor, cross water), (bridge, UsedFor, cross over), (bridge, ReceivesAction, find over river),*

A.1.3 "same rel, similar word"

- (cat, CapableOf, hunt mouse) : *(cat, CapableOf, hunt lizard), (cat, NotCapableOf, like mouse), (cat, UsedFor, kill mouse), (cat, CapableOf, kill mouse), (cat, Desires, eat mouse),*
- (pilot, CapableOf, land airplane) : *(pilot, CapableOf, carsh airplane), (pilot, CapableOf, land taildragger), (pilot, CapableOf, work in airplane), (pilot, CapableOf, land), (pilot, AtLocation, airplane),*
- (play sport, HasSubevent, run) : *(play baseball, HasSubevent, run), (play frisbee, Causes, run), (do some exercise, HasSubevent, run), (horse jump high when they, HasProperty, run), (go for run, HasSubevent, run),*

A.1.4 "different rel, similar word"

- (statue, AtLocation, museum) : *(statue, ReceivesAction, see in museum), (statue, IsA, example of art), (statue, UsedFor, imortalize someone), (statue, HasProperty, hard to create), (statue, CapableOf, be beautiful),*
- (son, PartOf, family) : *(son, IsA, member of family), (man and his daughter, IsA, family), (son, DefinedAs, child of parent), (son, AtLocation, his home), (son, IsA, male kid of his parent),*
- (internet, UsedFor, research) : *(internet, IsA, amaze research tool), (go on internet, UsedFor, research), (internet, IsA, research project of darpa), (internet, UsedFor, do research or chat), (internet, HasA, lot of information),*

A.1.5 "no directly related triple"

- (clerk, CapableOf, stock shelve) : *(clerk, CapableOf, be bag grocery), (clerk, CapableOf, price item), (clerk, CapableOf, bag grocery), (clerk, CapableOf, enter data), (clerk, AtLocation, at hotel),*
- (human, HasA, five finger on each hand) : *(human, HasA, five toe on each foot), (human, HasA, arm hand finger fingernail and lunula), (human, HasA, two hand), (human, CapableOf, write with right hand), (human, CapableOf, stand on two leg),*
- (cat, CapableOf, corner mouse) : *(cat, NotCapableOf, like mouse), (cat, CapableOf, kill mouse), (cat, UsedFor, kill mouse), (cat, UsedFor, keep mouse away), (cat, AtLocation, petstore),*

A.2 Random split

In this Section we report examples for novelty category from Random split dataset. For each example we include the 5 examples that were shown to the human annotator, ordered by closeness according to our word embedding metric.

A.2.1 "same rel, rephrase"

- (coffee mug, AtLocation, cupboard) : *(mug, AtLocation, cupboard), (coffee cup, AtLocation, cupboard), (tea cup, AtLocation, cupboard), (cup and plate, AtLocation, cupboard), (can of soup, AtLocation, cupboard),*

- (man, IsA, person) : *(man, IsA, male person), (egoistic person, IsA, person), (woman, IsA, person), (child, InheritsFrom, person), (child, IsA, person),*

- (bookshelf, IsA, for store book) : *(bookshelf, UsedFor, store book), (bookshelf, UsedFor, display and store read material), (bookshelf, UsedFor, hold and organize book), (bookshelf, UsedFor, organize book), (bookshelf, UsedFor, display book),*

A.2.2 "different rel, rephrase"

- (hear sing, HasSubevent, listen) : *(hear sing, HasFirstSubevent, listen), (hear sing, HasPrerequisite, listen), (hear, HasPrerequisite, listen), (hear music, HasPrerequisite, listen), (hear music, HasSubevent, listen),*

- (procreate, HasPrerequisite, find mate) : *(procreate, HasFirstSubevent, find mate), (procreate, Causes, have to raise your grandchild), (procreate, HasFirstSubevent, form will to do so),*

- (go outside for even, MotivatedByGoal, see star) : *(go outside for even, HasSubevent, that you see star), (go to film, UsedFor, see star), (go outside for even, UsedFor, look at star), (go outside for even, MotivatedByGoal, you have date), (go outside for even, UsedFor, get out of house),*

A.2.3 "same rel, similar word"

- (aluminum, IsA, metal) : *(aluminum, IsA, material), (safety-pins, MadeOf, metal), (titanium, IsA, metal), (quicksilver, IsA, metal), (plumbum, IsA, metal),*

- (cherry, AtLocation, jar) : *(vegemite, AtLocation, jar), (beet, AtLocation, jar), (toffee, AtLocation, jar), (jellybeans, AtLocation, jar), (moonshine, AtLocation, jar),*

- (u.s president, IsA, political leader) : *(u.s president, IsA, in charge of arm force), (president of something, IsA, it leader), (president, IsA, leader), (president, DefinedAs, leader of american government), (us president, IsA, important political figure),*

A.2.4 "different rel, similar word"

- (attach case, AtLocation, embassy) : *(attach case, UsedFor, carry paper and book), (attach case, AtLocation, office), (attach case, AtLocation, courtroom), (attache case, AtLocation, businessperson hand), (attache case, CapableOf, hold important document),*

- (catch mumps, Causes, sickness) : *(die, HasSubevent, sickness), (catch mumps, HasSubevent, you have fever), (catch mumps, HasFirstSubevent, get sick), (catch mumps, MotivatedByGoal, be sick), (cold, IsA, sickness),*

- (buy something for love one, Causes, get lay) : *(get in line, MotivatedByGoal, get lay), (have party, UsedFor, get lay), (get pay, UsedFor, get lay), (become inebriate, UsedFor, get lay),*

A.2.5 "no directly related triple"

- (fall from hot air balloon, CapableOf, kill you) : *(if you drink salt water it, CapableOf, kill you), (drink sea water, CapableOf, kill you), (water, CapableOf, kill you), (lighten, CapableOf, kill you), (pretty thing, CapableOf, kill you),*

- (milk, IsA, part of many food) : *(milk, DefinedAs, product of cow), (milk, ReceivesAction, produce by female cow), (milk, CapableOf, come from cow), (milk, ReceivesAction, make into cheese), (milk, ReceivesAction, create from cow),*

- (some food, ReceivesAction, make from dead animal) : *(some food, HasProperty, good but some be very dissgusting), (some food, IsA, healthy and some be not), (some food, HasProperty, poisonous if prepare improperly), (some food, ReceivesAction, grind before eat), (some food, HasProperty, consider exotic),*

A.3 Wikipedia

In this Section we report examples for novelty category from Wikipedia dataset. For each example we include the 5 examples that were shown to the human annotator, ordered by closeness according to our word embedding metric.

A.3.1 "same rel, rephrase"

- (deep snow, IsA, winter) : *(snow, SymbolOf, winter), (snow, AtLocation, winter), (it, IsA, winter), (snowflake, AtLocation, winter), (nice time of year, IsA, winter time),*

- (winter season, HasProperty, cold) : *(winter weather, HasProperty, cold), (in winter it, HasProperty, cold), (snow fall from sky when weather, HasProperty, cold), (stethascopes, HasProperty, cold), (cold weather, Causes, cold),*

- (mathematical logic, HasProperty, logical) : *(mathmatics, HasProperty, logical), (human wish for happiness but happiness, NotHasProperty, logical), (design computer chip, HasPrerequisite, logical think), (write program, HasPrerequisite, logical think), (logic, DefinedAs, set of rule by which axiom can be manipulate to derive true statement),*

A.3.2 "different rel, rephrase"

- (the house, HasA, room) : *(house, MadeOf, room), (many different way to put furniture, AtLocation, room), (something you find upstairs, IsA, room), (something you find downstairs, IsA, room), (family room, IsA, room),*

A.3.3 "same rel, similar word"

- (bus system, AtLocation, city) : *(subway system, AtLocation, city), (bus stop, AtLocation, city), (bus, AtLocation, city), (bus shelter, AtLocation, city), (bus station, AtLocation, city),*

- (satellite radio, HasA, channel) : *(tv, HasA, channel), (hear news, HasSubevent, change channel), (watch television, HasSubevent, change channel), (cnn, IsA, television channel), (cnn, IsA, tv channel),*

- (summer, IsA, hotter weather) : *(summer, HasA, more sunshine than winter), (summer, IsA, hot than winter), (summer, IsA, warm than winter), (summer, DefinedAs, season of baseball), (summer, DefinedAs, warm season),*

A.3.4 "different rel, similar word"

- (liberal democracy, HasProperty, political) : *(democracy, IsA, political system), (liberal democratic party, InstanceOf, japanese political party), (feminism, IsA, political ideology), (libertarianism, IsA, political ideology), (liberalism, IsA, political ideology),*

- (music, UsedFor, musical express) : *(music, CapableOf, be express use musical notation), (music, ReceivesAction, play with musical instrument), (music, ReceivesAction, write with musical symbol), (music, CreatedBy, instrument or human voice), (music, CapableOf, express feel),*

- (the planet, HasA, mass) : *(boston, PartOf, mass), (matter, HasA, mass), (planet plutoi, ReceivesAction, discover by mr), (some planet, HasA, more than one moon), (magnitude of planet, IsA, quantifiable),*

A.3.5 "no directly related triple"

- (field, HasA, vector potential) : *(field, HasA, plant grow in them), (field, UsedFor, agricultural pursuit), (field, UsedFor, cultivate crop), (field, UsedFor, graze livestock), (field, UsedFor, ride horse),*

- (town, HasA, center of commerce) : *(town, ReceivesAction, compose of many neighborhood), (town, HasProperty, likely to have several cafe), (town, IsA, small than city), (town, DefinedAs, prarie dog community), (town, UsedFor, live in),*

- (divorce, HasProperty, mutual consent) : *(divorce, NotHasProperty, more common than marriage), (divorce, DefinedAs, official end to marriage), (divorce, IsA, fact of life), (divorce, DefinedAs, termination of marriage), (divorce, IsA, when marry couple separate legallyt),*

Deep learning evaluation using deep linguistic processing

Alexander Kuhnle
Department of Computer Science
and Technology
University of Cambridge
aok25@cam.ac.uk

Ann Copestake
Department of Computer Science
and Technology
University of Cambridge
aac10@cam.ac.uk

Abstract

We discuss problems with the standard approaches to evaluation for tasks like visual question answering, and argue that artificial data can be used to address these as a complement to current practice. We demonstrate that with the help of existing 'deep' linguistic processing technology we are able to create challenging abstract datasets, which enable us to investigate the language understanding abilities of multimodal deep learning models in detail, as compared to a single performance value on a static and monolithic dataset.

1 Introduction & related work

In recent years, deep neural networks (DNNs) have established a new level of performance for many tasks in natural language processing (NLP), speech, computer vision and artificial intelligence. Simultaneously, we observe a move towards simulated environments and artificial data, particularly in reinforcement learning (Bellemare et al., 2013; Brockman et al., 2016). As outlined by Kiela et al. (2016), simulated data is appealing for various reasons. Most importantly, it acts as a prototypical problem presentation, abstracted from its noisy and intertwined real-world appearance.

However, with a few notable exceptions (Scheffler and Young, 2001; Byron et al., 2007), artificial data is relatively little used in NLP. Only recently people started arguing for the use of simulated data, like the long-term research proposal of Mikolov et al. (2015) on learning to understand language from scratch in a virtual environment, and introduced benchmark datasets, like the bAbI tasks (Weston et al., 2015) or the VQA datasets discussed below. Here we focus on the problem of *visually grounded language understanding* in the context of visual question answering (VQA). In principle, this task is particularly interesting from a semantic perspective, since it combines general language understanding, reference resolution and grounded language reasoning in a simple and clear task. However, recent work (Goyal et al., 2017; Agrawal et al., 2016) has suggested that the popular VQA Dataset (Antol et al., 2015) is inadequate, due to various issues which allow a system to achieve competitive performance without truly learning these abilities.

To address this, modifications to the existing VQA Dataset and several artificial VQA datasets have been released. The former include C-VQA (Agrawal et al., 2017), a new composition-focused split, and VQA 2.0 (Goyal et al., 2017), an extension based on minimal image pairs. Similar approaches have been proposed in the context of image captioning (Shekhar et al., 2017; Hodosh and Hockenmaier, 2016), which relate to our proposal in that they modify language in a principled way. However, despite 'mild artificiality', some issues with real-world data like the VQA Dataset remain.

On the other hand, examples of new artificial datasets include the SHAPES dataset (Andreas et al., 2016), the CLEVR dataset (Johnson et al., 2017a), the NLVR dataset (Suhr et al., 2017), and the ShapeWorld framework (Kuhnle and Copestake, 2017), which is our implementation of the proposal presented here. They all consist of images showing abstract scenes with colored objects and, except for NLVR, use artificially produced language. Language generation for SHAPES and CLEVR is template-based and dataset-specific, while ShapeWorld leverages an existing broad-coverage semantic grammar formalism.

These datasets are introduced with the motivation to provide a clear and challenging evaluation for VQA systems. Johnson et al. (2017a) and Kuhnle and Copestake (2017) investigated popular VQA systems on their datasets, and demonstrate how artificial data provides us with detailed

Proceedings of the Workshop on Generalization in the Age of Deep Learning, pages 17–23
New Orleans, Louisiana, June 5, 2018.

insights previously not possible. Despite its simplicity, they uncover fundamental shortcomings of current VQA models. Since then, CLEVR has been of great importance for the development of new VQA models based on dynamically assembled modules (Hu et al., 2017; Johnson et al., 2017b), a dedicated relational module (Santoro et al., 2017), or a general modulation technique (Perez et al., 2018), all of which achieve close-to-perfect accuracy on CLEVR.

The advantage of artificial data in this paper is not seen in its capacity to improve existing models by augmenting training data, although this would be conceivable. Instead we are interested in its capacity to provide data for targeted investigations of specific model capabilities. We argue that it constitutes a *necessary*, though not in itself *sufficient* benchmark for genuine language understanding abilities. The aforementioned models exhibit clearly superior understanding of the types of questions CLEVR contains. This paper proposes a principled way of continuing the incremental progress in multimodal language understanding initiated by CLEVR and its template-based generation approach, based on deep linguistic processing tools. Our initial experiments show that we can provide data that is challenging for state-of-the-art models, like the quantification examples presented in section 3.3. Note that while success on such narrower datasets may not directly translate to improved performance on broader datasets like the VQA Dataset, the underlying mechanisms are important for progress in the longer run.

Our aims in this paper are threefold. First, we provide a brief but systematic review of the problems surrounding current standard evaluation practices in deep learning. Secondly, we use this to motivate the potential of artificial data from simulated microworlds to investigate DNNs for visually grounded language understanding. Thirdly, we present an evaluation methodology based on linguistic processing resources, and show why compositional semantic representations from a symbolic grammar are particularly suitable for the production of artificial datasets.

2 Problems of real-world datasets

In the following, we review a variety of issues related to the practice of evaluating DNNs on popular real-world datasets for tasks like VQA. We emphasize that our arguments are mainly based on large-scale and broad-coverage datasets obtained in a relatively unconstrained way. Some of the points do not (fully) apply to more specific and carefully obtained data, like the NLVR dataset.

2.1 Issues with crowdsourced real-world data

The fact that DNNs require immense amounts of data for successful training led to the practice of adopting online data, such as the Flickr photo sharing platform, and leveraging crowdsourcing, usually via Amazon Mechanical Turk (AMT). For instance, the image captioning dataset MS COCO (Lin et al., 2014) contains more than 300,000 images annotated with more than 2 million human-written captions, while the popular VQA Dataset (Antol et al., 2015) is based on MS COCO.

Data obtained this way tends to be comparatively simple in terms of syntax and compositional semantics, despite exhibiting a high degree of lexical complexity due to its real-world breadth. Moreover, 're-purposed' photos do not – and were never intended to – reflect the visual complexity of every-day scenarios (Pinto et al., 2008). Humans given the task of captioning such images will mostly produce descriptions which are syntactically simple. The way that workers on crowdsourcing platforms are paid gives them an incentive to come up with captions quickly, and hence further increases the tendency to simplicity. Note also that, while this is a form of real-world data, it has very little relationship to the way that a human language learner perceives the world, from the fact that image/question pairs are presented in no meaningful order to the impossibility of any kind of interaction with a particular scene.

Natural language follows Zipf's law for many aspects (sentence length, syntactic complexity, word usage, etc), and consequently has an inbuilt simplicity bias when considered in terms of probability mass. The contents of image datasets based on photos also have a Zipfian distribution, but with biases which relate to what people choose to photograph rather than to what they see. Animal images in the VQA Dataset are predominantly cats and dogs, sport images mainly baseball and tennis (see Antol et al. (2015) for more statistics). Considering all these biases both in language and vision, the common evaluation measure – simple accuracy of questions answered correctly – is not a good reflection of a system's general ability to understand visually grounded language.

2.2 The Clever Hans effect

Crowdsourced visual questions have other unexpected properties. Goyal et al. (2017) and Mahendru et al. (2017) note how questions rarely talk about objects that are not present in the image, hence an existential question like *"Do you see a...?"* is mostly true. Agrawal et al. (2016) also give the example of questions like *"What covers the ground?"*, which can confidently be answered with *"snow"* because of biases in common real-world scenes, or, more precisely, biases in the photographs of real-world scenes. Such biases help to explain why some *text-only* systems turn out to perform well on *visual* question answering when evaluated on the VQA Dataset.

Sturm (2014) compared such unexpected cues when evaluation machine learning systems to the story of 'Clever Hans', a horse exhibited in the early 20th century which was claimed to understand German and have extensive arithmetical and reasoning abilities. Hans was eventually found to be picking up on very subtle cues which were given completely unconsciously by his owner and which were not noticed by ordinary observers. Some of the recent findings for DNNs, particularly in NLP, suggest similarly problematic conclusions, like the surprisingly strong performance of a bag-of-words model for sequential information (Adi et al., 2017) or of text-only systems for multimodal information (Jabri et al., 2016).

A more fundamental form of this effect is illustrated by recent investigations in image recognition. Szegedy et al. (2014) and Nguyen et al. (2015) have shown surprisingly odd system behavior when confronted with either only minimally modified images or almost random noise. This behavior seems due to the specific interplay of a few parameters which dominate the model's decision, and have led to an entire research subfield on adversarial instances in vision. Such investigations are not yet as prominent in the NLP community, although see, e.g., Jia and Liang (2017), Sproat and Jaitly (2016) and Arthur et al. (2016).

The ability to work with raw input data and to pick up correlations/biases, which humans cannot always manifest in explicit symbolic rules, is precisely the strength of DNNs as feature extractors. But given the often millions of parameters and large number of unstructured input values, it is difficult to avoid unexpected hidden cues. Real-world data with its enormous 'sample space', which is necessarily only sparsely reflected, is hence particularly prone to this effect.

The immediate problem is that a system trained this way may not generalize appropriately to other situations. The longer-term problem is that, while we do not expect that DNNs will simulate human capabilities in a fine-grained way, there has to be some degree of comparability if they are ever to be capable of justifying or explaining their behavior. The 'Clever Hans effect' thus refers to situations where we wrongly and prematurely attribute such human-like reasoning mechanisms to trained models, when more careful and systematic investigations would have revealed our misjudgement.

2.3 Guiding principles for DNN evaluation

Compositionality is a fundamental aspect of language, and consequently a necessary prerequisite for any claim about *'understanding'* natural language. Besides being required for proper generalization to novel utterances, it constitutes a far more efficient way of learning in the form of a structural prior, it leads to more interpretable inference results by forcing more systematic processing, and it results in more robust behavior, promising to reduce vulnerability to adversarial examples. However, Lake and Baroni (2017) recently gave reason to doubt the compositional capabilities of recurrent DNNs, which are at the heart of virtually all state-of-the-art NLP models. We conclude from this that a different kind of test data than existing benchmarks is required for more conclusive evaluations, and propose three simple principled ways to reduce the risk of encountering such problems:

- Avoid solely evaluating a system on a single and supposedly representative set, but design test instances with the aim of specifically investigating and confirming the system's intended improvement over other models.
- Instead of keeping training and test data distributions similar, focus on the true compositional generalization abilities required by dissimilar distributions. A more asymmetric dataset represents a harder, but hence potentially more interesting task.
- Do at least some experiments with clean data, which reduces the likelihood of hidden biases or correlations compared to more 'realistic' and complex data. For instance, the relationship between image and text should be explicitly controlled in multimodal data.

A pentagon is above a green ellipse, and no blue shape is an ellipse.

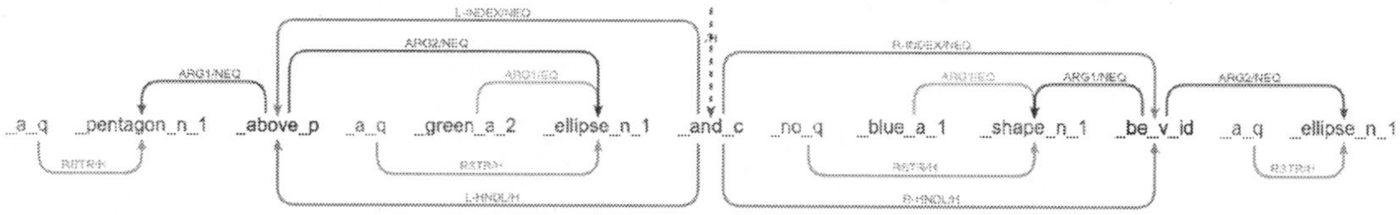

<table>
<tr><td>$\exists a$</td><td>a.shape=pg</td><td>a.y>b.y</td><td>$\exists b$</td><td>b.color=gr</td><td>b.shape=el</td><td>$\wedge$</td><td>$\neg\exists c$</td><td>c.color=bl</td><td>true</td><td>$c=d$</td><td>$\exists d$</td><td>d.shape=el</td></tr>
<tr><td colspan="2">$\exists a$: a.shape=pg</td><td>a.y>b.y</td><td colspan="3">$\exists b$: b.color=gr $\wedge$ b.shape=el</td><td>$\wedge$</td><td colspan="3">$\neg\exists c$: c.color=bl</td><td>$c=d$</td><td colspan="2">$\exists d$: d.shape=el</td></tr>
<tr><td colspan="6">$\exists a$: a.shape=pg $\wedge$ [$\exists b$: b.color=gr $\wedge$ b.shape=el $\wedge$ a.y>b.y]</td><td>$\wedge$</td><td colspan="6">$\neg\exists c$: c.color=bl $\wedge$ [$\exists d$: d.shape=el $\wedge$ $c=d$]</td></tr>
<tr><td colspan="13">($\exists a$: a.shape=pg $\wedge$ [$\exists b$: b.color=gr $\wedge$ b.shape=el $\wedge$ a.y>b.y]) $\wedge$ ($\neg\exists c$: c.color=bl $\wedge$ [$\exists d$: d.shape=el $\wedge$ $c=d$])</td></tr>
</table>

Figure 1: A caption with DMRS graph and semantic interpretation, illustrating how compositionality enables us to generate combinatorially large amounts of non-trivial captions and infer their semantics from atomic elements.

3 Automatic generation of language data

In the following, we describe our approach for automatic generation of artificial VQA data using existing deep linguistic processing technology, based on our implementation in the ShapeWorld framework (Kuhnle and Copestake, 2017)[1]. We argue that a compositional semantic approach using a bidirectional grammar gives us precisely the sort of data as outlined by the above principles. We propose this approach as a complementary evaluation step, since it is not intended to replace real-world evaluation, but instead aims to cover aspects which existing datasets cannot provide.

3.1 Abstract microworlds

The generation process we use is based on randomly sampled abstract world models, i.e. values which specify a microworld, entities and all their attributes. In the case of our framework these include the number of entities, their shape and color, position, rotation, shade, etc. Such a world model can be visualized straightforwardly.

In this context, datasets are generators which can create an unlimited amount of data instances, hence making multiple iterations over a fixed set of training instances obsolete. Importantly, different datasets constrain the general sampling process in different ways by, for instance, restricting the number of objects, the attribute values available, the positioning of entities, and more. This addresses the point of specifying different data distributions for training and testing. Moreover, it makes it possible to partition evaluation data as desired, which facilitates the detailed investigation of system behavior for specific instances and hence the discovery of systematic shortcomings.

[1]https://github.com/AlexKuhnle/ShapeWorld

3.2 Syntactically rich language generation

Of the recent abstract datasets mentioned in the introduction, Suhr et al. (2017) use human-written captions, the SHAPES dataset (Andreas et al., 2016) a minimalist grammar, and the CLEVR dataset (Johnson et al., 2017a) a more complex one based on functional building blocks, both template-based and specifically designed for their data. For our approach we leverage technology made available by the DELPH-IN (Deep Linguistic Processing with HPSG) consortium. More specifically, we make use of the broad-coverage, bidirectional[2], high-precision English Resource Grammar (Flickinger, 2000), which builds on the compositional semantic framework of Minimal Recursion Semantics (Copestake et al., 2005). For our system we use one of its variant, Dependency MRS (DMRS, Copestake (2009), Copestake et al. (2016)), and generate natural language sentences from abstract DMRS graphs using Packard's parser-generator ACE[3].

We have found that DMRS graphs can easily be enriched with appropriate semantics to be evaluated on a given world model. This means that the internals of the language system are essentially using a form of model-theoretic semantics. However, the external presentation of our task is still *'natural'*, i.e. only consists of image and language. Compositional representations like DMRS further enable us to produce an infinite number of captions of arbitrary syntactic complexity.

Figure 1 shows an example of a non-trivial caption with corresponding DMRS graph and logical representation over a world model. Both the

[2]Bidirectional grammars can be used for generation as well as parsing, of which the latter might be useful here, for instance, in investigating ambiguity effects.

[3]http://sweaglesw.org/linguistics/ace/

- Less than one triangle is cyan.
- At least half the triangles are red.
- More than a third of the shapes are cyan squares.
- Exactly all the five squares are red.
- More than one of the seven cyan shapes is a cyan square.
- Twice as many red shapes as yellow shapes are circles.

Figure 2: An image with several example captions focusing on quantification. The task is image caption agreement, that is, to decide whether the caption agrees with the image (green) or not (red), similar to yes/no questions in VQA.

abstractness and compositionality of the semantic representation are essential to allow us to scale beyond toy examples. The abstract scenario puts an emphasis on experiments with closed-class vocabulary and syntax, as compared to open-class dominated real-world datasets. However, the same approach can be extended to more complex domains, like the clip-arts of Zitnick et al. (2016).

In the future, we plan to implement two interesting extensions for our framework: First, paraphrase rules can be expressed on grammar-level and integrated into the generation process as post-processing step for increased linguistic variety. Second, (D)MRS-based grammars for other languages, such as the JACY grammar for Japanese (Siegel et al., 2016), can be used simply by translating the internal mapping of atomic DMRS components to corresponding semantic elements.

3.3 Quantification example

Figure 2 presents an example image accompanied by a variety of correct and incorrect captions focusing on quantification. We produce both count-based (*"three"*) and fraction-based (generalized) quantifiers (*"half"*) in various modifications (*"less than three"*), optionally with additional number restriction (*"at least three of the five"*) or comparative (*"half as many as"*).

We decide to focus on quantifiers here because, on the one hand, they can exhibit a high degree of structural complexity, which can only be resolved by using visual information. On the other hand, categories like 'number' in VQA 2.0 or 'count' and 'compare integer' in CLEVR imply that count-based quantification is specifically covered by these datasets. As the various captions in figure 2 illustrate, this is not fully the case. Note that we so far do not consider scope ambiguity of nested quantifiers, although our approach can be extended accordingly, since the (D)MRS formalism supports scope underspecification, which is one of the reasons for choosing DMRS.

4 Conclusion: Why use artificial data?

Challenging test data. The interplay of abstract world model and semantic language representation enables us to generate captions requiring non-trivial multimodal reasoning. In fact, the resulting captions can be more complex than the sort of captions we could plausibly obtain from humans, and do not suffer from a Zipfian tendency to simplicity on average (unless configured accordingly).

Avoid Clever Hans effect. The simple, abstract domain and the controlled generation process based on randomly sampling microworlds makes such data comparatively unbiased and greatly reduces the possibility of hidden complex correlations. We can be confident that we cover the data space both relatively uniformly and more exhaustively than this is the case in real-world datasets.

Flexibility & reusability. Real-world and/or human-created data essentially has to be obtained again for every change/update, like for VQA v2.0 (Goyal et al., 2017). In contrast to that, modularity and detailed configurability make our approach easily reusable for a wide range of potentially unforeseen changes in evaluation focus.

Rich evaluation. Ultimately, our goal in providing datasets is to enable detailed evaluations (of DNNs). By creating atomic test datasets specifically evaluating instance types individually (e.g., counting, spatial relations, or even more fine-grained), we can unit-test a DNN for specific subtasks. We believe that such a modular approach is a better way to establish trust in the understanding abilities of DNNs than a monolithic dataset and a single accuracy number to assess performance.

Acknowledgments

We thank the anonymous reviewers for their constructive feedback. AK is grateful for being supported by a Qualcomm Research Studentship and an EPSRC Doctoral Training Studentship.

References

Yossi Adi, Einat Kermany, Yonatan Belinkov, Ofer Lavi, and Yoav Goldberg. 2017. Fine-grained analysis of sentence embeddings using auxiliary prediction tasks. In *Proceedings of the International Conference on Learning Representations*, ICLR 2017.

Aishwarya Agrawal, Dhruv Batra, and Devi Parikh. 2016. Analyzing the behavior of visual question answering models. In *Proceedings of the Conference on Empirical Methods in Natural Language Processing*, EMNLP 2016, pages 1955–1960.

Aishwarya Agrawal, Aniruddha Kembhavi, Dhruv Batra, and Devi Parikh. 2017. C-VQA: A compositional split of the visual question answering (VQA) v1.0 dataset. *CoRR*, abs/1704.08243.

Jacob Andreas, Marcus Rohrbach, Trevor Darrell, and Dan Klein. 2016. Neural module networks. In *Proceedings of the IEEE Conference on Computer Vision and Pattern Recognition*, CVPR 2016.

Stanislaw Antol, Aishwarya Agrawal, Jiasen Lu, Margaret Mitchell, Dhruv Batra, C. Lawrence Zitnick, and Devi Parikh. 2015. VQA: Visual question answering. In *Proceedings of the IEEE International Conference on Computer Vision*, ICCV 2015.

Philip Arthur, Graham Neubig, and Satoshi Nakamura. 2016. Incorporating discrete translation lexicons into neural machine translation. In *Proceedings of the Conference on Empirical Methods in Natural Language Processing*, EMNLP 2016.

Marc G. Bellemare, Yavar Naddaf, Joel Veness, and Michael Bowling. 2013. The arcade learning environment: An evaluation platform for general agents. *Journal of Artificial Intelligence Research*, 47(1):253–279.

Greg Brockman, Vicki Cheung, Ludwig Pettersson, Jonas Schneider, John Schulman, Jie Tang, and Wojciech Zaremba. 2016. OpenAI Gym.

Donna Byron, Alexander Koller, Jon Oberlander, Laura Stoia, and Kristina Striegnitz. 2007. Generating instructions in virtual environments (GIVE): A challenge and an evaluation testbed for NLG. In *Proceedings of the Workshop on Shared Tasks and Comparative Evaluation in Natural Language Generation*.

Ann Copestake. 2009. Slacker semantics: Why superficiality, dependency and avoidance of commitment can be the right way to go. In *Proceedings of the 12th Meeting of the European Chapter of the Association for Computational Linguistics*, EACL 2009, pages 1–9.

Ann Copestake, Guy Emerson, Michael W. Goodman, Matic Horvat, Alexander Kuhnle, and Ewa Muszyńska. 2016. Resources for building applications with Dependency Minimal Recursion Semantics. In *Proceedings of the 10th International Conference on Language Resources and Evaluation*, LREC 2016, pages 1240–1247.

Ann Copestake, Dan Flickinger, Carl Pollard, and Ivan A. Sag. 2005. Minimal Recursion Semantics: An introduction. *Research on Language and Computation*, 3(4):281–332.

Dan Flickinger. 2000. On building a more efficient grammar by exploiting types. *Natural Language Engineering*, 6(1):15–28.

Yash Goyal, Tejas Khot, Douglas Summers-Stay, Dhruv Batra, and Devi Parikh. 2017. Making the V in VQA matter: Elevating the role of image understanding in Visual Question Answering. In *Proceedings of the IEEE Conference on Computer Vision and Pattern Recognition*, CVPR 2017, pages 6325–6334.

Micah Hodosh and Julia Hockenmaier. 2016. Focused evaluation for image description with binary forced-choice tasks. In *Proceedings of the 5th Workshop on Vision and Language*, pages 19–28.

Ronghang Hu, Jacob Andreas, Marcus Rohrbach, Trevor Darrell, and Kate Saenko. 2017. Learning to reason: End-to-end module networks for visual question answering. In *Proceedings of the IEEE International Conference on Computer Vision*, ICCV 2017.

Allan Jabri, Armand Joulin, and Laurens van der Maaten. 2016. Revisiting visual question answering baselines. In *Proceedings of the 14th European Conference on Computer Vision*, ECCV 2016, pages 727–739.

Robin Jia and Percy Liang. 2017. Adversarial examples for evaluating reading comprehension systems. In *Proceedings of the Conference on Empirical Methods in Natural Language Processing*, EMNLP 2017, pages 2021–2031.

Justin Johnson, Bharath Hariharan, Laurens van der Maaten, Li Fei-Fei, C. Lawrence Zitnick, and Ross Girshick. 2017a. CLEVR: A diagnostic dataset for compositional language and elementary visual reasoning. In *Proceedings of the IEEE Conference on Computer Vision and Pattern Recognition*, CVPR 2017.

Justin Johnson, Bharath Hariharan, Laurens van der Maaten, Judy Hoffman, Li Fei-Fei, C Lawrence Zitnick, and Ross Girshick. 2017b. Inferring and executing programs for visual reasoning. In *Proceedings of the IEEE International Conference on Computer Vision*, ICCV 2017.

Douwe Kiela, Luana Bulat, Anita L. Vero, and Stephen Clark. 2016. Virtual embodiment: A scalable long-term strategy for artificial intelligence research. *CoRR*, abs/1610.07432.

Alexander Kuhnle and Ann Copestake. 2017. Shapeworld - A new test methodology for multimodal language understanding. *CoRR*, abs/1704.04517.

Brenden M. Lake and Marco Baroni. 2017. Still not systematic after all these years: On the compositional skills of sequence-to-sequence recurrent networks. *CoRR*, abs/1711.00350.

Tsung-Yi Lin, Michael Maire, Serge Belongie, James Hays, Pietro Perona, Deva Ramanan, Piotr Dollár, and C. Lawrence Zitnick. 2014. Microsoft COCO: Common objects in context. In *Proceedings of the European Conference on Computer Vision*, ECCV 2014.

Aroma Mahendru, Viraj Prabhu, Akrit Mohapatra, Dhruv Batra, and Stefan Lee. 2017. The promise of premise: Harnessing question premises in visual question answering. In *Proceedings of the Conference on Empirical Methods in Natural Language Processing*, EMNLP 2017.

Tomas Mikolov, Armand Joulin, and Marco Baroni. 2015. A roadmap towards machine intelligence. *CoRR*, abs/1511.08130.

Anh Nguyen, Jason Yosinski, and Jeff Clune. 2015. Deep neural networks are easily fooled: High confidence predictions for unrecognizable images. In *Proceedings of the IEEE Conference on Computer Vision and Pattern Recognition*, CVPR 2015.

Ethan Perez, Florian Strub, Harm de Vries, Vincent Dumoulin, and Aaron C. Courville. 2018. FiLM: Visual reasoning with a general conditioning layer. In *AAAI*.

Nicolas Pinto, David D. Cox, and James J. DiCarlo. 2008. Why is real-world visual object recognition hard? *PLOS Computational Biology*, 4(1):1–6.

Adam Santoro, David Raposo, David G. T. Barrett, Mateusz Malinowski, Razvan Pascanu, Peter Battaglia, and Timothy P. Lillicrap. 2017. A simple neural network module for relational reasoning. In *Advances in Neural Information Processing Systems 30: Annual Conference on Neural Information Processing Systems*, NIPS 2017, pages 4974–4983.

Konrad Scheffler and Steve Young. 2001. Corpus-based dialogue simulation for automatic strategy learning and evaluation. In *Proceedings of the NAACL Workshop on Adaptation in Dialogue Systems*, pages 64–70.

Ravi Shekhar, Sandro Pezzelle, Yauhen Klimovich, Aurélie Herbelot, Moin Nabi, Enver Sangineto, and Raffaella Bernardi. 2017. FOIL it! Find one mismatch between image and language caption. In *Proceedings of the 55th Annual Meeting of the Association for Computational Linguistics*, ACL 2017, pages 255–265.

Melanie Siegel, Emily M. Bender, and Francis Bond. 2016. *Jacy: An Implemented Grammar of Japanese*. CSLI Studies in Computational Linguistics. CSLI Publications, Stanford, California, USA.

Richard Sproat and Navdeep Jaitly. 2016. RNN approaches to text normalization: A challenge. *CoRR*, abs/1611.00068.

Bob L. Sturm. 2014. A simple method to determine if a music information retrieval system is a "horse". *IEEE Transactions on Multimedia*, 16(6):1636–1644.

Alane Suhr, Mike Lewis, James Yeh, and Yoav Artzi. 2017. A corpus of natural language for visual reasoning. In *55th Annual Meeting of the Association for Computational Linguistics*, ACL 2017.

Christian Szegedy, Wojciech Zaremba, Ilya Sutskever, Joan Bruna, Dumitru Erhan, Ian J. Goodfellow, and Rob Fergus. 2014. Intriguing properties of neural networks. *CoRR*, abs/1312.6199.

Jason Weston, Antoine Bordes, Sumit Chopra, and Tomas Mikolov. 2015. Towards AI-complete question answering: A set of prerequisite toy tasks. *CoRR*, abs/1502.05698.

C. Lawrence Zitnick, Ramakrishna Vedantam, and Devi Parikh. 2016. Adopting abstract images for semantic scene understanding. *IEEE Transactions on Pattern Analysis and Machine Intelligence*, 38(4):627–638.

The Fine Line between Linguistic Generalization and Failure in Seq2Seq-Attention Models

Noah Weber*, **Leena Shekhar***, **Niranjan Balasubramanian**
Stony Brook University, NY
{nwweber, lshekhar, niranjan}@cs.stonybrook.edu

Abstract

Seq2Seq based neural architectures have become the go-to architecture to apply to sequence to sequence language tasks. Despite their excellent performance on these tasks, recent work has noted that these models usually do not fully capture the linguistic structure required to generalize beyond the dense sections of the data distribution (Ettinger et al., 2017), and as such, are likely to fail on samples from the tail end of the distribution (such as inputs that are noisy (Belinkov and Bisk, 2018) or of different lengths (Bentivogli et al., 2016)). In this paper, we look at a model's ability to generalize on a simple symbol rewriting task with a clearly defined structure. We find that the model's ability to generalize this structure beyond the training distribution depends greatly on the chosen random seed, even when performance on the standard test set remains the same. This suggests that a model's ability to capture generalizable structure is highly sensitive. Moreover, this sensitivity may not be apparent when evaluating it on standard test sets.

1 Introduction

It is well known that language has certain structural properties which allows natural language speakers to make "infinite use of finite means" (Chomsky, 1965). This structure allows us to generalize beyond the typical machine learning definition of generalization (Valiant, 1984) (which considers performance on the distribution that generated the training set), permitting the understanding of any utterance sharing the same structure, regardless of probability. We refer to this notion as *linguistic* generalization [1].

Many problems in NLP are treated as sequence to sequence tasks with solutions built on seq2seq-attention based models. While these models perform very well on standard datasets and also appear to capture some linguistic structure (Williams et al., 2018; Belinkov et al., 2017; Linzen et al., 2016), they also can be quite brittle, typically breaking on uncharacteristic inputs (Lake and Baroni, 2018; Belinkov and Bisk, 2018).

Due to the high capacity of these models, it is not unreasonable to expect them to learn *some* structure from the data. However, learning structure is not a sufficient condition to achieving linguistic generalization. If this structure is to be usable on data outside the training distribution, the model must learn the structure *without* additionally learning patterns specific to the training data.

In this work, we look at the feasibility of training seq2seq-attention models so they generalize in this linguistic sense. We train models on a symbol replacement task with a well defined generalizable structure. The task is simple enough that all models achieve near perfect accuracy on the standard test set, i.e., where the inputs are drawn from the same distribution as that of the training set. We then test these models for linguistic generalization by creating test sets of uncharacteristic inputs, i.e., inputs that are not typical in the training distribution but still solvable given that the generalizable structure was learned. Our results show that generalization is highly sensitive[2]; even changes in the random seed can drastically affect the ability to generalize. This suggests that the line between generalization and failure is quite fine, and may not be feasible to reach by tuning alone.

2 Symbol Rewriting Task

Real world NLP tasks are complex, and as such, it can be difficult to precisely define what a model

*These authors contributed equally to this work.

[1] From here on, mentions of generalization refer to the linguistic kind.

[2] The sensitivity of generalization is also hinted at in McCoy et al. (2018) who additionally note performance variations across initializations

Proceedings of the Workshop on Generalization in the Age of Deep Learning, pages 24–27
New Orleans, Louisiana, June 5, 2018.

should and should not learn during training. As done in previous work (Lake and Baroni, 2018; Rodriguez and Wiles, 1998), we ease analysis by looking at a simple formal task. The task is set up to mimic (albeit, in an oversimplified manner) the input-output symbol alignments and local syntactic properties that models must learn in many natural language tasks, such as translation, tagging and summarization. The task is defined over sequences of symbols, $\{x_1, ...x_n | x_i \in X\}$, where X is the input alphabet. Each symbol $x \in X$ is uniquely associated with its own output alphabet Y_x. Output is created by taking each individual symbol x_i in the sequence and rewriting it as any sequence of k symbols from Y_{x_i}. To do the task, the model must learn alignments between the input and output symbols, and preserve the simple local syntactic conditions (every group of k symbols must come from the same input alphabet Y_x). As an example, let $X = \{A, B\}$, $Y_A = \{\text{Consonants}\}$, $Y_B = \{\text{Vowels}\}$, and $k = 2$. Then a valid output for the input BA would be $aupt$. For our task, $|X| = 40$ and each x_i has a corresponding output alphabet Y_{x_i} of size 16.

To generalize to any input sequence, a model must: **(1)** learn the generalizable structure - the alignments between input and output alphabets, and **(2)** *not* learn any dependencies among input symbols or sequence length. To test the extent to which **(2)** is met, we train[3] seq2seq-attention models with 100,000 randomly generated samples with inputs uniformly generated with lengths 5-10 and no input symbol appearing more than once in a single sample. If the model learned alignments without picking up other dependencies among input symbols or input lengths then the resulting model should have little problem in handling inputs with repeated symbols or different lengths, despite never seeing such strings.

For evaluation we trained 50 different models with the *same* configuration, chosen with a validation set, but with *different* random seeds. We created 4 different test sets, each with 2000 randomly generated samples. The first test set consists of samples that are characteristic of the training set, having lengths 5-10 and no repeats (**Standard**). The second set tests the model's ability to generalize to repeated symbols in the input (**Repeat**). The third and fourth sets test its ability to generalize to different input lengths, strings of length 1-4 (**Short**) and 11-15 (**Long**) respectively.

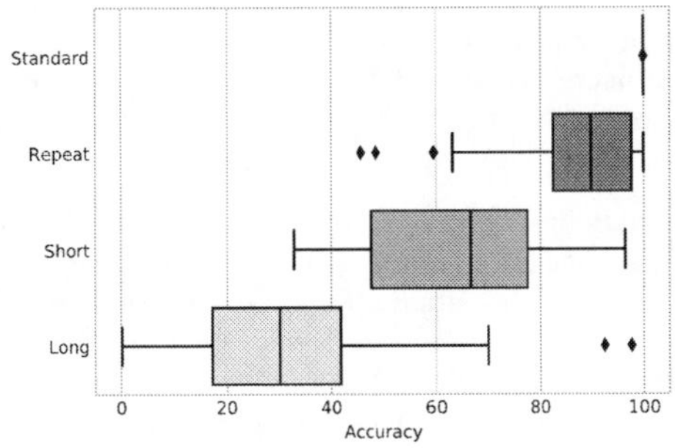

Figure 1: Accuracy % distribution across 50 runs with different random seeds on the four test sets.

3 Results and Conclusions

The distribution of model accuracy[4] measured at instance level on the four test sets across all the 50 seeds is given in Figure 1. All models perform above 99% on the standard set, with a deviation well below 0.1. However, the deviation on the other two sets is much larger, ranging from 13.39 for the repeat set to 20.63 for the long set. In general, the model performs better on the repeat set than on the short and long sets. Performance on the short and long sets is not always bad, some seeds giving performances of above 95% for either the short or long set. Ideally, we would like a seed which performs good on all the test sets; however, this seems hard to obtain. The highest average performance across the non standard test sets for any seed was 79.52%. Learning to generalize for both the repeated and longer inputs seems even harder, with the Pearson correlation between performance on the repeat and long sets being -0.71.

The variability in generalization on uncharacteristic inputs (and thus, the extent of linguistic generalization) given different random seeds is alarming, particularly given the fact that the standard test set performance remains mostly the same regardless. The task presented here was easy and simple to analyze, however, future work may be done on natural language tasks. If these properties hold it might indicate that a new evaluation paradigm for NLP should be pushed; one that emphasizes performance on uncharacteristic inputs in addition to the data typically seen in training.

[3]A detailed account of model training, regularization, and tuning is provided in the supplementary material.

[4]We compute accuracy as $\frac{\text{\# times the model produced a valid output}}{\text{\# samples}}$.

References

Yonatan Belinkov and Yonatan Bisk. 2018. Synthetic and natural noise both break neural machine translation. *6th International Conference on Learning Representations* .

Yonatan Belinkov, Nadir Durrani, Fahim Dalvi, Hassan Sajjad, and James Glass. 2017. What do neural machine translation models learn about morphology? In *Proceedings of the 55th Annual Meeting of the Association for Computational Linguistics (Volume 1: Long Papers)*. Association for Computational Linguistics, pages 861–872.

Luisa Bentivogli, Arianna Bisazza, Mauro Cettolo, and Marcello Federico. 2016. Neural versus phrase-based machine translation quality: a case study. In *Proceedings of the 2016 Conference on Empirical Methods in Natural Language Processing*. Association for Computational Linguistics, pages 257–267.

Noam Chomsky. 1965. *Aspects of the Theory of Syntax*. The MIT Press, Cambridge.

Allyson Ettinger, Sudha Rao, Hal Daum III, and Emily M Bender. 2017. Towards linguistically generalizable nlp systems: A workshop and shared task. In *Proceedings of the First Workshop on Building Linguistically Generalizable NLP Systems*.

Sepp Hochreiter and Jürgen Schmidhuber. 1997. Long short-term memory. *Neural Comput.* 9(8):1735–1780.

Brenden Lake and Marco Baroni. 2018. Still not systematic after all these years: On the compositional skills of sequence-to-sequence recurrent networks. *ICLR 2018* .

Tal Linzen, Emmanuel Dupoux, and Yoav Goldberg. 2016. Assessing the ability of lstms to learn syntax-sensitive dependencies. *TACL* 4:521–535.

Thang Luong, Hieu Pham, and Christopher D. Manning. 2015. Effective approaches to attention-based neural machine translation. In *EMNLP*. The Association for Computational Linguistics, pages 1412–1421.

R. Thomas McCoy, Robert Frank, and Tal Linzen. 2018. Revisiting the poverty of the stimulus: hierarchical generalization without a hierarchical bias in recurrent neural networks. *CoRR* abs/1802.09091.

Paul Rodriguez and Janet Wiles. 1998. Recurrent neural networks can learn to implement symbol-sensitive counting. In *Advances in Neural Information Processing Systems*. pages 87–93.

L. G. Valiant. 1984. A theory of the learnable. *Commun. ACM* 27(11):1134–1142.

Adina Williams, Andrew Drozdov, and Samuel R. Bowman. 2018. Do latent tree learning models identify meaningful structure in sentences? *Transactions of the ACL (TACL)* abs/1709.01121.

A Supplemental Material

A.1 Model and Training Details

The models we use are single layer, unidirectional, seq2seq LSTMs (Hochreiter and Schmidhuber, 1997) with bilinear attention (Luong et al., 2015) and trained with vanilla SGD. To determine the epoch to stop training at, we create a validation set of 2000 samples with the same characteristics as the training set, i.e., of length 5-10 with no repeated symbols. Training is stopped once accuracy[5] on the validation set either decreases or remains unchanged. The size of the hidden state and embeddings were chosen such that they were as small as possible without reducing validation accuracy, giving a size of 32.

Tuning hyperparameters is often done on a validation set drawn from the same distribution as the training set (as we often don't know the exact form of uncharacteristic inputs, with the exception of noisy inputs) which motivated our decision to use a validation set of characteristic inputs to decide the epoch to stop at. However, we noticed only small variation in the validation performance upon using different learning rates and dropout probabilities (where dropout was applied to the input and output layers). In order to fine tune these parameters to avoid extreme overfitting, we created another validation set consisting of 5000 samples of "uncharacteristic" inputs, i.e., inputs with repeated symbols and varying from length 3-12. These two hyperparameter values were set to 0.125 and 0.1, respectively, according to the performance on this validation set, averaged across a set of randomly chosen random seeds. Further training details are listed in Table 1.

A.2 Symbol Rewriting Task Examples

Here we provide a simple example of the task. If the input symbol A maps to any permutations of a_1, a_2, or a_3, and B maps to permutations of b_1, b_2, or b_3. Each a_i and b_i has 2 possible values, a_{i1} or a_{i2} and b_{i1} or b_{i2} respectively. Thus, mapping an input symbol to 48 ($8 * 3!$) possible permutations. A possible valid output for the input AB is $a_{21}a_{32}a_{11}b_{32}b_{11}b_{22}$. Note that any such permutation is valid and permutations are selected at random when generating the data. We allow this stochasticity in the outputs in order to prevent the model from resorting to pure memorization. Ta-

[5] Defined in section 3

LSTM Layers	1
WE/LSTM size	32
Attention	Bilinear
Batch size	64
Optimizer	SGD
LR	0.125
Max gradient norm	5
Dropout	0.1

Table 1: Model details.

	Standard	Repeat	Short	Long
Size	2k	2k	2k	2k
Src Length	5-10	5-10	1-4	11-15
Tgt Length	15-30	15-30	3-12	33-45

Table 2: Details about the four test sets used in our experiments.

ble 2 provides further information on the 4 different test sets.

A.3 Model Performance

We provide the summary statistics across all runs (50 different random seeds) in Table 3, which gives the mean, standard deviation, minimum, and maximum accuracies across all random seeds. We additionally provide a sample of performances for some individual random seeds in Table 4, with the highest and lowest accuracies in each column highlighted.

	Standard	Repeat	Short	Long
Mean	99.85	86.67	64.36	32.09
Std.	0.03	13.39	18.61	20.63
Min.	99.73	45.70	32.80	0.15
Max.	99.88	99.85	96.35	97.60

Table 3: Accuracy % summarized across all 50 runs with different random seeds.

Seed	Standard	Repeat	Short	Long
2787	**99.88**	94.65	42.05	23.05
5740	99.86	**45.70**	56.55	**97.60**
10000	99.86	98.55	**32.80**	**0.15**
14932	**99.73**	87.05	42.20	29.75
28897	99.87	**99.85**	47.40	1.40
30468	99.87	86.35	**96.35**	12.90

Table 4: Accuracy % on the test sets for selected runs out of 50 with different random seeds.

Extrapolation in NLP

Jeff Mitchell, Pasquale Minervini, Pontus Stenetorp and **Sebastian Riedel**
University College London
Department of Computer Science
{j.mitchell, p.minervini, p.stenetorp, s.riedel}@cs.ucl.ac.uk

Abstract

We argue that extrapolation to examples outside the training space will often be easier for models that capture global structures, rather than just maximise their local fit to the training data. We show that this is true for two popular models: the Decomposable Attention Model and word2vec.

1 Introduction

In a controversial essay, Marcus (2018a) draws the distinction between two types of generalisation: *interpolation* and *extrapolation*; with the former being predictions made *between* the training data points, and the latter being generalisation *outside* this space. He goes on to claim that deep learning is only effective at interpolation, but that human like learning and behaviour requires extrapolation.

On Twitter, Thomas Diettrich rebutted this claim with the response that no methods extrapolate; that *what appears to be extrapolation from X to Y is interpolation in a representation that makes X and Y look the same.* [1]

It is certainly true that extrapolation is hard, but there appear to be clear real-world examples. For example, in 1705, using Newton's then new inverse square law of gravity, Halley predicted the return of a comet 75 years in the future. This prediction was not only possible for a new celestial object for which only a limited amount of data was available, but was also effective on an orbital period twice as long as any of those known to Newton. Pre-Newtonian models required a set of parameters (deferents, epicycles, equants, etc.) for each body and so would struggle to generalise from known objects to new ones. Newton's theory of gravity, in contrast, not only described celestial orbits but also predicted the motion of bodies thrown or dropped on Earth.

[1] https://twitter.com/tdietterich/status/948811920001282049

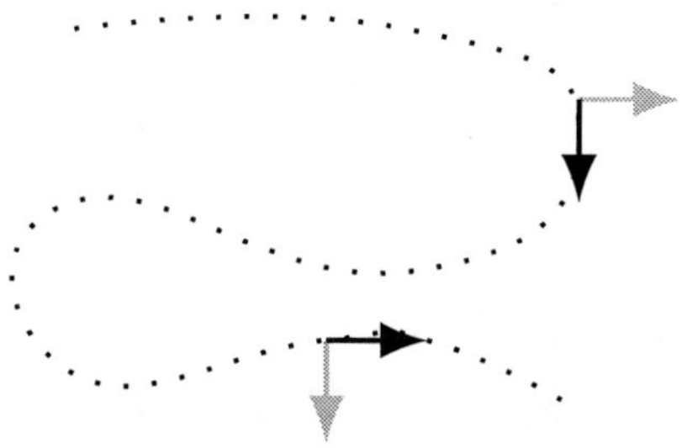

Figure 1: Generalising to unseen data: dotted line = training manifold; black arrows = interpolation; grey arrows = extrapolation. Both directions are represented globally in the training data, but local interpolation is only effective in one of them at each point.

In fact, most scientists would regard this sort of extrapolation to new phenomena as a vital test of any theory's legitimacy. Thus, the question of what is required for extrapolation is reasonably important for the development of NLP and deep learning.

Marcus (2018a) proposes an experiment, consisting of learning the identity function for binary numbers, where the training set contains only the even integers but at test time the model is required to generalise to even numbers. A standard multilayer perceptron (MLP) applied to this data fails to learn anything about the least significant bit in input and output, as it is constant throughout the training set, and therefore fails to generalise to the test set. Many readers of the article ridiculed the task and questioned its relevance. Here, we will argue that it is surprisingly easy to solve Marcus' even-odd task and that the problem it illustrates is actually endemic throughout machine learning.

Marcus (2018a) links his experiment to the systematic ways in which the meaning and use of a word in one context is related to its meaning and

Proceedings of the Workshop on Generalization in the Age of Deep Learning, pages 28–33
New Orleans, Louisiana, June 5, 2018. ©2018 Association for Computational Linguistics

use in another (Fodor and Pylyshyn, 1988; Lake and Baroni, 2017). These regularities allow us to extrapolate from sometimes even a single use of a word to understand all of its other uses.

In fact, we can often use a symbol effectively with no prior data. For example, a language user that has never have encountered the symbol *Socrates* before may nonetheless be able to leverage their syntactic, semantic and inferential skills to conclude that *Socrates is mortal* contradicts *Socrates is not mortal*.

Marcus' experiment essentially requires extrapolating what has been learned about one set of symbols to a new symbol in a systematic way. However, this transfer is not facilitated by the techniques usually associated with improving generalisation, such as L2-regularisation (Tikhonov, 1963), drop-out (Srivastava et al., 2014) or preferring flatter optima (Hochreiter and Schmidhuber, 1995).

In the next section, we present four ways to solve this problem and discuss the role of global symmetry in effective extrapolation to the unseen digit. Following that we present practical examples of global structure in the representation of sentences and words. Global, in these examples, means a model form that introduces dependencies between distant regions of the input space.

2 Four Ways to Learn the Identity Function

The problem is described concretely by Marcus (1998), with inputs and outputs both consisting of five units representing the binary digits of the integers zero to thirty one. The training data consists of the binary digits of the even numbers $(0, 2, 4, 8, \ldots, 30)$ and the test set consists of the odd numbers $(1, 3, 5, 7, \ldots, 31)$. The task is to learn the identity function from the training data in a way that generalises to the test set.

The first model (SLP) we consider is a simple linear single layer perceptron from input to output.

In the second model (FLIP), we employ a change of representation. Although the inputs and outputs are given and fixed in terms of the binary digits **1** and **0**, we will treat these as symbols and exploit the freedom to encode these into numeric values in the most effective way for the task. Specifically, we will represent the digit **1** with the number `0` and the digit **0** with the number `1`. Again, the network will be a linear single layer perceptron without biases.

Model	Train	Test
SLP	8.12e-06	0.99
FLIP	6.79e-05	1.04e-05
ORTHO	1.27e-04	4.09e-05
CONV	1.71e-04	3.20e-05
PROJ	5.15e-06	8.07e-06

Table 1: Mean Squared Error on the Train (even numbers) and Test (odd numbers) Sets.

Returning to the original common-sense representation, **1** $\rightarrow$ `1` and **0** $\rightarrow$ `0`, the third model (ORTHO) attempts to improve generalisation by imposing a global condition on the matrix of weights in the linear weights. In particular, we require that the matrix is orthogonal, and apply the absolute value function at the output to ensure the outputs are not negative.

For the fourth model (CONV), we use a linear Convolutional Neural Network (ConvNet, Lecun et al., 1998) with a filter of width five. In other words, the network weights define a single linear function that is shifted across the inputs for each output position.

Finally, in our fifth model (PROJ) we employ another change of representation, this time a dimensionality reduction technique. Specifically, we project the 5-dimensional binary digits $\mathbf{d}$ onto an n dimensional vector $\mathbf{r}$ and carry out the learning using an n-to-n layer in this smaller space.

$$\mathbf{r} = \mathbf{A}\mathbf{d} \tag{1}$$

where the entries of the matrix $\mathbf{A}$ are $A_{ij} = e^{\beta(j-i)}$. In each case, our loss and test evaluation is based on squared error between target and predicted outputs.

Training. Each model is implemented in TensorFlow (Abadi et al., 2015) and optimised for 1,000 epochs. In Eq. (1), we find that values of $\beta = \ln(2)$ and $n = 1$ work well in practice.

Results. As can be seen in Table 1, SLP fails to learn a function that generalises to the test set. In contrast, all the other models (FLIP, ORTHO, CONV, PROJ) generalise almost perfectly to the test set. Thus, we are left with four potential approaches to learning the identity function. Is lowest test set error the most appropriate means of choosing between them?

Discussion. This decision probably isn't as momentous as the choice discussed by Galileo in his Dialogue Concerning the Two Chief World Systems, where he presented the arguments for and against the heliocentric and geocentric models of planetary motion. These pre-Newtonian models could, in principle, attain as much predictive accuracy as desired, given enough data, by simply incorporating more epicycloids for each planet. On the other hand, they could not extrapolate beyond the bodies in that training data. Here, we will try to extract something useful from our results by considering how each model might generalise to other data and problems.

Although FLIP has the second lowest test set error, it is at best a cheap hack[2] which works only in the limited circumstance of this particular problem. If there were more than a single fixed digit in the training data, this trick would not work.

ORTHO suffers from the same problem, though it does embody the principle that everything in the input should end up in the output which seems to be part of this task.

CONV on the other hand will generalise to any size of input and output, and will even generalise to multiplication by powers of 2, rather than just learning the identity function.

PROJ, with the values $\beta = \ln(2)$ and $n = 1$, boils down to converting the binary digits into the equivalent single real value and learning the identity function via linear regression. This approach will extrapolate to values of any magnitude[3] and generalise to learning any linear function, rather than just the identity. As such, it is probably the only practically sensible solution, although it cheats by avoiding the central difficulty in the original problem.

At its most general, this central difficulty is the problem of extrapolating in a direction that is perpendicular to the training manifold. The even number inputs lay on a 4 dimensional subspace, while the odd numbers were displaced in a direction at right angles to that subspace. In this general form, the problem of how to respond to variation in the test set that is perpendicular to the training manifold lacks a well-defined unique solution, and this helps to explain why many people dismissed the task entirely.

However, this problem is in fact pervasive in most of machine learning. Training instances will typically lie on a low dimensional manifold and effective generalisation to new data sources will commonly require handling variation that is orthogonal to that manifold in an appropriate manner, e.g. Fig. 1. If prediction is based on local interpolation using a highly non-linear function, then no amount of smoothing of the fit will help.

Convolution is able to extrapolate from even to odd numbers because it exploits the key structure of the ordering of digits that a human would use. A human, given this task, would recognise the correspondence between input and output positions and then apply the same copying operation at each digit, which is essentially what convolution learns to do. It implicitly assumes that there is a global translational symmetry[4] across input positions, and this reduces the number of parameters and allows generalisation from one digit to another.

Returning to the linguistic question that inspired the task, we can think of systematicity in terms of symmetries that preserve the meaning of a word or sentence (Kiddon and Domingos, 2015). Ideally, our NLP models should embody or learn the symmetries that allow the same meaning to be expressed within multiple grammatical structures.

Unfortunately, syntax is complex and prohibits a short and clear investigation here. On the other hand, relations between sentences (e.g. contradiction) sometimes have much simpler symmetries. In the next section, we examine how global symmetries can be exploited in an inference task.

3 Global Symmetries in Natural Language Inference

The Stanford Natural Language Inference (SNLI, Bowman et al., 2015) dataset attempts to provide training and evaluation data for the task of categorising the logical relationship between a pair of sentences. Systems must identify whether each hypothesis stands in a relation of *entailment*, *contradiction* or *neutral* to its corresponding premise. A number of neural net architectures have been

[2]Nonetheless, such tricks are hardly unknown in machine learning research.

[3]Generalisation to values outside the training set would not be so successful had we used an MLP rather than a uniform linear function. Fitting to the training set using sigmoids will not yield a function that continues to approximate the identity very far beyond its range in the training set.

[4]Coincidentally, the rejection of the Earth centred model in favour of planetary motions orbiting the Sun played an important role in the recognition that the laws of physics also have a global translational symmetry, i.e. that no point in space is privileged or special.

proposed that effectively learn to make test set predictions based purely on patterns learned from the training data, without additional knowledge of the real world or of the logical structure of the task.

Here, we evaluate the Decomposable Attention Model (DAM, Parikh et al., 2016) in terms of its ability to extrapolate to novel instances, consisting of contradictions from the original test set which have been reversed. For a human that understands the task, such generalisation is obvious: knowing that A contradicts B is equivalent to knowing that B contradicts A. However, it is not at all clear that a model will learn this symmetry from the SNLI data, without it being imposed on the model in some way. Consequently we also evaluate a modification, S-DAM, where this constraint is enforced by design.

Models. Both models build representations, $\mathbf{v}_p$ and $\mathbf{v}_h$, of premise and hypothesis in attend and compare steps. The original DAM model then combines these representations by concatenating them and then transforming and aggregating the result to produce a final representation $\mathbf{u}_{ph}$, forming the input to a 3-way softmax:

$$\begin{aligned} \mathbf{u}_{ph} &= t(\mathbf{v}_p; \mathbf{v}_h), \\ p(i) &= s(\mathbf{u}_{ph} \cdot \mathbf{W}_i), \quad \text{with } i \in \{c, e, n\}. \end{aligned} \tag{2}$$

In S-DAM, we break the prediction into two decisions: contradiction vs. non-contradiction followed by entailment vs. neutral. The first decision is symmetrised by concatenating the vectors in both orders and then summing the output of the same transformation applied to both concatenations:

$$\begin{aligned} \tilde{\mathbf{u}}_{ph} &= t(\mathbf{v}_p; \mathbf{v}_h) + t(\mathbf{v}_h; \mathbf{v}_p), \\ p(j) &= s(\tilde{\mathbf{u}}_{ph} \cdot \tilde{\mathbf{W}}_j), \quad \text{with } j \in \{c, \neg c\}. \end{aligned} \tag{3}$$

Predictions for entailment and neutral are then made conditioned on $\neg c$:

$$\begin{aligned} \bar{\mathbf{u}}_{ph} &= t(\mathbf{v}_p; \mathbf{v}_h), \\ p(k|\neg c) &= s(\bar{\mathbf{u}}_{ph} \cdot \bar{\mathbf{W}}_k), \quad \text{with } k \in \{e, n\}. \end{aligned} \tag{4}$$

Results. Table 2 gives the accuracies for both models on the whole SNLI test set, the subset of contradictions, and the same set of contradictions reversed. In the last row, the DAM model suffers a significant fall in performance when the contradictions are reversed. In comparison, the S-DAM's performance is almost identical on both sets.

Instances	DAM	S-DAM
Whole Test Set	86.71%	85.95%
Contradictions	85.94%	85.69%
Reversed Contradictions	78.13%	85.20%

Table 2: Accuracy on all instances, contradictions and reversed contradictions from the SNLI test set.

Thus, the S-DAM model extrapolates more effectively because its architecture exploits a global symmetry of the relation between sentences in the task. In the following section, we investigate a global symmetry within the representation of words.

4 Global Structure in Word Embeddings

Word embeddings, such as GloVe (Pennington et al., 2014) and word2vec (Mikolov et al., 2013), have been enormously effective as input representations for downstream tasks such as question answering or natural language inference. One well known application is the $king = queen - woman + man$ example, which represents an impressive extrapolation from word co-occurrence statistics to linguistic analogies (Levy and Goldberg, 2014). To some extent, we can see this prediction as exploiting a global structure in which the differences between analogical pairs, such as $man - woman$, $king - queen$ and $father - mother$, are approximately equal.

Here, we consider how this global structure in the learned embeddings is related to a linearity in the training objective. In particular, linear functions have the property that $f(a + b) = f(a) + f(b)$, imposing a systematic relation between the predictions we make for a, b and $a + b$. In fact, we could think of this as a form of translational symmetry where adding a to the input has the same effect on the output throughout the space.

We hypothesise that breaking this linearity, and allowing a more local fit to the training data will undermine the global structure that the analogy predictions exploit.

Models. These embedding models typically rely on a simple dot product comparison of target and context vectors as the basis for predicting some measure of co-occurrence s:

$$s = f\left(\sum_i \text{target}_i \cdot \text{context}_i\right). \tag{5}$$

D	Linear	Non-Linear
100	50.38%	42.96%
200	53.18%	40.66%
400	50.77%	32.43%

Table 3: Accuracy on the analogy task.

We replace this simple linear function of the context vectors, with a set of non-linear broken-stick functions $g_i(\cdot)$.

$$s = f\left(\sum_i g_i\left(\text{context}_i\right)\right),$$

$$g_i(x) = \begin{cases} m_i x & \text{if } n_i x + c_i < 0, \\ (m_i + n_i)\, x + c_i & \text{otherwise.} \end{cases}$$

We modify the CBOW algorithm in the publicly available word2vec code to incorporate this non-linearity and train on the commonly used *text8* corpus of 17M words from Wikipedia. As this modification doubles the number of parameters used for each word, we test models of dimensions 100, 200 and 400.

Results. Table 3 reports the performance on the standard analogy task distributed with the word2vec code. The non-linear modification of CBOW is substantially less successful than the original linear version on this task. This is true on all the sizes of models we evaluated, indicating that this decrease is not simply a result of over-parameterisation.

Thus, destroying the global linearity in the embedding model undermines extrapolation to the analogy task.

5 Conclusions

Language is a very complex phenomenon, and many of its quirks and idioms need to be treated as local phenomena. However, we have also shown here examples in the representation of words and sentences where global structure supports extrapolation outside the training data.

One tool for thinking about this dichotomy is the *equivalent kernel* (Silverman, 1984), which measures the extent to which a given prediction is influenced by nearby training examples. Typically, models with highly local equivalent kernels - e.g. splines, sigmoids and random forests - are preferred over non-local models - e.g. polynomials - in the context of general curve fitting (Hastie et al., 2001).

However, these latter functions are also typically those used to express fundamental scientific laws - e.g. $E = mc^2$, $F = G\frac{m_1 m_2}{r^2}$ - which frequently support extrapolation outside the original data from which they were derived. Local models, by their very nature, are less suited to making predictions outside the training manifold, as the influence of those training instances attenuates quickly.

We suggest that NLP will benefit from incorporating more global structure into its models. Existing background knowledge is one possible source for such additional structure (Marcus, 2018b; Minervini et al., 2017). But it will also be necessary to uncover novel global relations, following the example of the other natural sciences.

We have used the development of the scientific understanding of planetary motion as a repeated example of the possibility of uncovering global structures that support extrapolation, throughout our discussion. Kepler and Newton found laws that went beyond simply maximising the fit to the known set of planetary bodies to describe regularities that held for every body, terrestrial and heavenly.

In our SNLI example, we showed that simply maximising the fit on the development and test sets does not yield a model that extrapolates to reversed contradictions. In the case of word2vec, we showed that performance on the analogy task was related to the linearity in the objective function.

More generally, we want to draw attention to the need for models in NLP that make meaningful predictions outside the space of the training data, and to argue that such extrapolation requires distinct modelling techniques from interpolation within the training space. Specifically, whereas the latter can often effectively rely on local smoothing between training instances, the former may require models that exploit global structures of the language phenomena.

Acknowledgments

The authors are immensely grateful to Ivan Sanchez Carmona for many fruitful disagreements. This work has been supported by the European Union H2020 project SUMMA (grant No. 688139), and by an Allen Distinguished Investigator Award.

References

Martín Abadi, Ashish Agarwal, Paul Barham, Eugene Brevdo, Zhifeng Chen, Craig Citro, Greg S. Corrado, Andy Davis, Jeffrey Dean, Matthieu Devin, Sanjay Ghemawat, Ian Goodfellow, Andrew Harp, Geoffrey Irving, Michael Isard, Yangqing Jia, Rafal Jozefowicz, Lukasz Kaiser, Manjunath Kudlur, Josh Levenberg, Dandelion Mané, Rajat Monga, Sherry Moore, Derek Murray, Chris Olah, Mike Schuster, Jonathon Shlens, Benoit Steiner, Ilya Sutskever, Kunal Talwar, Paul Tucker, Vincent Vanhoucke, Vijay Vasudevan, Fernanda Viégas, Oriol Vinyals, Pete Warden, Martin Wattenberg, Martin Wicke, Yuan Yu, and Xiaoqiang Zheng. 2015. TensorFlow: Large-scale machine learning on heterogeneous systems. Software available from tensorflow.org.

Samuel R. Bowman, Gabor Angeli, Christopher Potts, and Christopher D. Manning. 2015. A large annotated corpus for learning natural language inference. In *Proceedings of the 2015 Conference on Empirical Methods in Natural Language Processing (EMNLP)*. Association for Computational Linguistics.

Jerry A. Fodor and Zenon W. Pylyshyn. 1988. Connectionism and cognitive architecture. *Cognition*, 28(1-2):3–71.

Trevor Hastie, Robert Tibshirani, and Jerome Friedman. 2001. *The Elements of Statistical Learning*. Springer Series in Statistics. Springer New York Inc., New York, NY, USA.

Sepp Hochreiter and Jrgen Schmidhuber. 1995. Simplifying neural nets by discovering flat minima. In *Advances in Neural Information Processing Systems 7*, pages 529–536. MIT Press.

Chloé Kiddon and Pedro Rauel Cândido Domingos. 2015. Symmetry-based semantic parsing. Https://homes.cs.washington.edu/ pedrod/papers/sp14.pdf.

B. M. Lake and M. Baroni. 2017. Generalization without systematicity: On the compositional skills of sequence-to-sequence recurrent networks. *ArXiv e-prints*.

Yann Lecun, Lon Bottou, Yoshua Bengio, and Patrick Haffner. 1998. Gradient-based learning applied to document recognition. In *Proceedings of the IEEE*, pages 2278–2324.

Omer Levy and Yoav Goldberg. 2014. Linguistic regularities in sparse and explicit word representations. In *Proceedings of the Eighteenth Conference on Computational Natural Language Learning, CoNLL 2014*, pages 171–180.

G. Marcus. 2018a. Deep Learning: A Critical Appraisal. *ArXiv e-prints*.

G. Marcus. 2018b. Innateness, AlphaZero, and Artificial Intelligence. *ArXiv e-prints*.

Gary F. Marcus. 1998. Rethinking eliminative connectionism. *Cognitive Psychology*, 37:243–282.

Tomas Mikolov, Ilya Sutskever, Kai Chen, Greg Corrado, and Jeffrey Dean. 2013. Distributed representations of words and phrases and their compositionality. In *Proceedings of the 26th International Conference on Neural Information Processing Systems - Volume 2*, NIPS'13, pages 3111–3119, USA. Curran Associates Inc.

Pasquale Minervini, Thomas Demeester, Tim Rocktäschel, and Sebastian Riedel. 2017. Adversarial sets for regularising neural link predictors. In *Proceedings of the Thirty-Third Conference on Uncertainty in Artificial Intelligence, UAI 2017, Sydney, Australia, August 11-15, 2017*. AUAI Press.

Ankur P. Parikh, Oscar Täckström, Dipanjan Das, and Jakob Uszkoreit. 2016. A decomposable attention model for natural language inference. In *Proceedings of the 2016 Conference on Empirical Methods in Natural Language Processing, EMNLP 2016, Austin, Texas, USA, November 1-4, 2016*, pages 2249–2255.

Jeffrey Pennington, Richard Socher, and Christopher D. Manning. 2014. Glove: Global vectors for word representation. In *In EMNLP*.

B. W. Silverman. 1984. Spline smoothing: The equivalent variable kernel method. *Ann. Statist.*, 12(3):898–916.

Nitish Srivastava, Geoffrey Hinton, Alex Krizhevsky, Ilya Sutskever, and Ruslan Salakhutdinov. 2014. Dropout: A simple way to prevent neural networks from overfitting. *Journal of Machine Learning Research*, 15:1929–1958.

A. N. Tikhonov. 1963. Solution of incorrectly formulated problems and the regularization method. *Soviet Math. Dokl.*, 4:1035–1038.

Author Index

Association for Computational Linguistics
209 N. Eighth Street
Stroudsburg, Pennsylvania 18360

ISBN 978-1-5108-6359-0

CURRAN ASSOCIATES INC.
proceedings.com